THE STRATEGIC *Bookkeeper*

My secret sauce recipe to creating a thriving practice by becoming a strategic bookkeeper

JEANNIE SAVAGE

The Strategic Bookkeeper
Jeannie Savage

First published in Australia by Jeannie Savage 2023
www.thestrategicbookkeeper.global

A catalogue record for this
book is available from the
National Library of Australia

ISBN: 978-0-6456951-0-6 (pbk)
ISBN: 978-0-6456951-1-3 (ebk)

Typesetting and design by Publicious Book Publishing
Published in collaboration with
Publicious Book Publishing
www.publicious.com.au

Special Acknowledgements & Dedications

This book is dedicated to my little red sheep and apple, my son Rory – always remember you're not ordinary, you're extraordinary.

Special Acknowledgements

My mother and father – by far the toughest bosses I ever had – thank you for the lessons, the opportunities and the love.

Contents

Chapter 1: Welcome to Becoming a Strategic Bookkeeper 1
Chapter 2: Your Brand 27
Chapter 3: Your menu.. 49
Chapter 4: The Power of Client Attraction 71
Chapter 5: The Process of Conversion........... 150
Chapter 6: The Joy of Succession.................... 177
Chapter 7: The Beauty of Systems. 206
Chapter 8: The Strength of Teams. 228

Chapter 1. Welcome to Becoming a Strategic Bookkeeper.

At the time of writing this book I'm traveling through Europe while my wonderful boutique team is taking care of business – I'm living my dream on my terms – which is what I want for you.

Hi, I'm Jeannie. I really appreciate you taking the time to read my work, and to show my appreciation I intend to help you transform yourself from being an ordinary bookkeeper (not that there's anything wrong with that) to becoming a strategic bookkeeper.

It's not a big, scary transformation at all. In fact it's a lot of fun, because you'll be venturing into all kinds of areas that are new and fascinating, and you'll be growing your business as you do it. Even more, my secret sauce can help you change other aspects of your life as well. I'm pretty certain that it will add value to everything you do. I know that's a big call, but I stand by it because I have that much faith in what I have to tell you, and in you as well.

In fact, I'm going to put my money where my mouth is: I hereby guarantee that this book will save or make you money (or both), and if you find that it doesn't, I'll happily give you the purchase price back.

The only catch is that you have to give my secret sauce a chance to work. You'll have to put some effort in, and at times you'll need to slip out of your comfort zone. But I promise it will be worth it, and I'd love it if you share your experiences with me once your transformation is complete.

Before we start, a few words about the "words & phrases" I'll be using.

I've spent a lot of time and invested a lot of money into developing the unique mode of thought leadership that you'll find in this book. As you read on, you'll be introduced to a whole range of terms, acronyms, concepts and methods that will help you in your journey to becoming a strategic bookkeeper. There are a few key ideas here that I think you should familiarise yourself with now, so it all makes sense as we go along.

Everything has the meaning we give it.

The first thing to remember is that everything has the meaning we give it. In other words, you are the master of your own destiny. You can control the way you think and feel about things. And in this book, I'm going to challenge you to redefine some words and phrases in order to build your confidence and help you see how capable you really are.

Part of the reason for this is to help you shift your mindset from feeling and thinking, "I'm not comfortable with this, I'm not good at this," especially around sales and marketing, to more positive and powerful self-talk.

Time and time again I've spoken with bookkeepers who've said to me, "Jeannie, I'm not comfortable with this, I'm not good at this." And I know where they're coming from, but the truth is, when you say that to yourself, in a way you're setting yourself up for failure.

You can never exceed your own expectations.

If you keep telling yourself you're "not the kind of person" to do certain things, you'll never do them. You need to reset your expectations...

"Let's turn your current ceiling into your new floor."

I know it's easy to say that, but I hope that as you read this book, you'll realise that you are capable of doing anything and everything that I have done. Just knowing that gives you a kind of freedom that money can't buy.

It's all about the long game.

There is no silver bullet. No quick fix. No one simple ingredient that will suddenly make all the difference in a month or two or even three. The truth is that to build or renovate your bookkeeping practice to a point where it's scaled up and thriving, you need to educate yourself thoroughly and then step by step implement what you learn, testing and measuring along the way.

I'd go one further and say that you might also need someone (or more than one) to support you along the way. And right now, that's my job. You and I are about to embark on a journey of true transformation, and that, my friend, takes time. A year to be precise.

Laps around the sun.

This is a phrase I've learnt to use with my clients and now I want to use it with you. Any major transformation, end to end, takes a year – a lap around the sun. And then, year on year, as you do more laps, you'll refine and grow and you'll deepen your success.

Will you get runs on the board in the early days? Hell yes! But the real rewards will come if you play the long game.

Rinse and repeat.

As a trainer and assessor, I understand that repetition is one of the most powerful paths to clarity and progress. With seven key principles to learn, and the myriad of details around implementing all of them, it's going to be vital to go back over old ground until the whole process is second nature to you. To *rinse and repeat* whenever necessary.

One more thing before we start.

As well as writing this book and hosting a podcast, I have developed The Strategic Bookkeeper Transformation Program. You'll find links in this book to find out more but for now, the most important thing you need to know is about the "done for you" elements of my program.

As you progress through the book, I'll give you activities to do and "assets" to build. If you elect to join my program, it's important you know that many of these will be served up "done for you".

In each chapter I'll do my best to point out what is done for you – so you're informed, and you can choose between DIY and done for you.

The program is a 12 month journey (a lap around the sun) and here are the five keys to how we make it work for you:

1. **Education:** As a trainer & assessor I'm passionate about ensuring you thoroughly learn what you need to know – and that you keep learning.

2. **Assets:** Most of the "Digital Assets" you'll learn to create in this book will be "done for you" – assets in every discipline - brand, menu, attraction, conversion, succession, systems and team – please look out for further explanation throughout the book.

3. **Implementation:** Once you've got the knowledge & assets my team and I will then help you implement it all step by step – testing and measuring your results, supporting you to make it all work in your practice.

4. **Team:** You'll harness the power of our group and gain immediate access to our team – imagine if you could hire a world-class marketing strategist, brand expert, put me on your team and more – This power can't reasonably be achieved as "one", but it can through the power of "many".

5. **Support:** You'll become a member of our "tribe" – a global community of Strategic Bookkeepers with a common purpose – you'll collaborate with and learn from each other – you'll network - you'll form mastermind groups, meet regularly and hold each other accountable to moving the needle.

Okay. With all that said, it's time to get down to tin tacks. Even if you think you'd be better off joining my tribe and getting my team to do a lot of the work for you, I still recommend reading through this book thoroughly – in fact, you'll get more out of my program if you do. Let's go.

What is a strategic bookkeeper?

Seven thousand years ago, Mesopotamian traders began making markings on clay tablets to keep track of how many bulls they had traded, loaves of bread they'd bartered, and jars they'd bought. These ancient markings are proof that bookkeeping is one of the oldest and most significant professions in the world.

Today, bookkeepers are essential workers in any successful business, recording all the transactions the business makes, and providing the data that managers need to make decisions around pretty much everything. Our industry keeps every other industry afloat, and without us chaos would quickly consume the economic landscape.

But many of us, probably even a majority, are stuck with the idea that we are simply "humble bookkeepers". And if that's the way you see yourself, that's the way others will see you as well. That will all change for you when you become a strategic bookkeeper.

A strategic bookkeeper is...

...someone who uses all the tools and strategies she has at her disposal to:

- ✓ Create business.
- ✓ Make her clients feel special and appreciative of her value.
- ✓ Ensure that her business is successful enough that she can, if she chooses, pay less attention to it and pursue other dreams.

A strategic bookkeeper is someone who understands and wields the tools that are crucial to finding, keeping and recruiting clients as her advocates, and to providing the services that keep those clients loyal. Every chapter in this book deals with one of those tools, so I've made it as easy as possible to become a strategic bookkeeper.

Where's the benefit to the client, Jeannie?

That is an excellent question, and it proves that you've been paying attention. So far, I've talked a lot about what you need to do to become a strategic bookkeeper, but not why that will appeal to your clients. So here goes.

Your value to your clients is not just in the diligent bookkeeping you bring into their business – it's in the *intelligence* you can provide. The numbers have a huge story to tell, and you can help interpret that story by shining a light on the numbers in a strategic way. That means:

- Slowly educating your clients around what the numbers mean because compared to you, they're in kindergarten when it comes to this stuff.
- Helping them to understand and perhaps reorganise the way they view their income and expenses so that the story becomes clearer to them over time.
- Helping them find out how they compare to their peers (with industry benchmarks readily available online from the tax office).
- Showing them how to set new targets based on these benchmarks.
- Teaching them how to monitor their actual business performance by sitting down regularly and being accountable to the numbers.

Which all adds up to helping them improve their business performance by making and saving money – as I'll show you in the Succession chapter.

OMG Jeannie, are you talking about giving clients *advice*???

The short answer is no – but remember when I said that everything has the meaning we give it?

What meaning have you attached to "advice"?

The truth is that we all give our clients advice every day – advice we're comfortable with, advice that's "in our lane". Anytime we tell our clients *what we need or what they need to do* – we're actually giving them advice.

The key here is that I'm never going to suggest you give advice you're not comfortable giving and in fact, as you read on, you'll discover that this is primarily about these 3 things:

- Shining a light on the numbers
- Powerful questions
- Being a facilitator

We'll cover this off in more detail in the succession chapter. For now, I strongly recommend that you put any fears around "giving advice" aside and allow me to walk you through my entire method before passing judgement.

As a Strategic Bookkeeper, you're no longer a cost - you're an investment!

It takes a lot to get to the point where you have all the pieces of the puzzle to confidently offer a strategic bookkeeping service, but that's the journey I am offering you. You'll learn how to apply the intelligence that was always there in the numbers, and to market yourself as a "value-added" bookkeeper – a strategic bookkeeper.

Why become a strategic bookkeeper?

Apart from the very real benefits being a strategic bookkeeper can deliver to your clients, the advantages it brings to you are enormous.

Over the years, I've met a lot of bookkeepers and it seems that the same problems beset every one of us at one time or another. These problems are:

1. Trouble finding new clients.
2. Difficulty retaining clients long term – *for the life of their business.*
3. Competing on price – and cost focussed clients.
4. Clients undervaluing your work, skills and contribution.

5. Competing with cheap overseas labour.
6. Staying relevant in a world of automation, AI and now, robotics
7. Developing the right systems and team

Becoming a strategic bookkeeper is about overcoming these problems. It's about creating rules, systems and habits to ensure that problems like these become much less business-threatening and more easily solved than you thought possible.

Becoming a strategic bookkeeper is about taking control of your destiny, and building your success brick by brick, day by day, client by client. It's an exciting and invigorating journey, and one that I have proven can succeed.

No more hourly rates.

There are many bookkeepers who are still charging by the hour – but that's not what a strategic bookkeeper does. We sell outcomes, not time. And our clients love it.

Is moving to fixed-price (aka value-billing) the solution to all your problems? No. But it's a principle and it's pillar – and it's a pricing system you need to adopt if you're going to be a Strategic Bookkeeper in Practice.

The key here is you making the leap to recognising that when you sell your *time by the hour,* you're doing yourself a disservice and I'd argue you're using a broken business model. Your strategic bookkeeping skills add huge value to your clients' businesses and provide them with *priceless "peace of mind".*

You become an asset to their business and they become willing to pay not just for your time, but your value. And that will change your life.

But Jeannie, why secret sauce?

As you read this book, you'll find that I do things a bit differently and the results are surprising, wholesome and fulfilling, adding life and zest to the business of doing business for you and your clients. "Secret sauce" is my way of flagging that with you from the beginning.

Whenever I meet a new client, I ask them "what's your secret sauce? What makes your business a success?" Their answers give me an insight into how they do things and why, and help me understand their systems.

So I realised it was time to fully understand and document my own secret sauce – the systems, processes, ideas and approaches that have helped me create and sustain my successful practice.

A lot of my systems have been built through trial and error, and my team and I have worked really hard to refine our procedures and methods to the point where they deliver outstanding results for my clients. So I took the time to step back and take stock of it all, and map it out as a way to pass on my experience and thought leadership. The 7 ingredients in my secret sauce recipe are Brand, Menu, Attraction, Conversion, Succession, Systems and Team.

What it means for you.

When you employ my principles, you'll get more joy out of every day, because my techniques will make your life easier and more organised, and everything you do will yield more satisfying results.

When we develop your unique *Brand Building Playbook,* we'll delve into *your* secret sauce, and that will be one of the primary bases of your own journey to becoming a strategic bookkeeper. We'll put together a step by step program that will include all the ingredients you need to be a success, and give you the systems you need to make it happen – because we all know how much we bookkeepers love a system.

It doesn't matter whether you're just starting out on your journey as a bookkeeper or you have a thriving practice, there is something for every bookkeeper in the world in my method. Even if you think you know it all, I am willing to bet the price of this book that you'll learn something new, whether it's in the area of branding, attraction, conversion, succession, or any other section.

How do I know that? Because whatever you're going through with your business, I've been through it. I've been on a long road to get where I am today and I've learned a lot of lessons the hard way, so you don't have to.

My story.

They say working mums never take a break, especially if they work from home. And that is absolutely my experience. But I've managed to work it so that my business life remains successful and expands without imposing on my most important job, which is being a mother.

Let's go back to 2010, when I had my little boy. I already had two beautiful stepchildren, adorable ten year old twins, but along came my own child, and my life changed. It was amazing to me, and it still is, just how much love I am able to pour into the little person my partner and I made together, and right from the start I decided that whatever I did next was going to have to fit around my gorgeous child.

I ended up having a special needs child, so that made it even more important that I spend time with my child, and more rewarding.

Know thyself.

I've always believed that one of the keys to success is for us to really understand what drives us, and I've put a lot of effort into that over the years. One of the tools I've used here is the *Human Needs Test*, which I learned about from listening to Tony Robbins, and according to that my primary human needs are growth and contribution. They're my top two human needs and I'm really driven to grow every day and to contribute to people. I love to help other people grow as well, which is one of the reasons I'm here at a keyboard, writing this book. It's a goal of mine to create a community of bookkeepers – a tribe – by reaching out to help as many of my fellow professionals as possible.

I strongly recommend that you take a few minutes to take Tony's easy ten question test – you can find it here: https://core.tonyrobbins.com/driving-force-6/.

You may also consider the wealth dynamics test, which is available at https://wealthdynamics.geniusu.com/ and the free online DISC personality test at https://www.onlinepersonalitytests.org/disc/.

Anyway, that's just a little side piece I thought I would share with you – so back to my story.

My parents' business.

I'd done a lot of different things in my life up to the point that my baby came along, and one of the most important and rewarding things was working in my parents' business. That's because it taught me a lot, and it was incredibly successful: I helped them to scale their business from $10 million to $100 million. I didn't do that all by myself, of course, there were lots of us involved, but my contribution was real and it was a really amazing life lesson.

My job was to go into the departments that weren't working as they should – and let me tell you, some were in real trouble – and figure out what the problems were. So I would look at them and say to myself, how does this need to be reorganised, and how can I prioritise what needs to be done? I developed quite a system, and I would recruit staff, train them in the system, stay around long enough to see that it was all working properly, and then move on to the next department.

The time I spent helping my parents to expand their business was important to me because it gave me my love of scaling, and it showed me how it can be done and what the rewards are. But I also learned about every single aspect of running a business, so it gave me a great insight into how all those aspects work together.

How I started my practice.

Fast forward to 2009 and the arrival of my baby, and I had a choice to make. What work would I do that I found stimulating, but would also be flexible enough so that I would be able to spend as much time as I needed just being a mama? If possible, this work should also be scalable, so that I could build something bigger than me.

I chose to concentrate on bookkeeping, because it's about numbers, which I love, but also because it's important. And it's something I could do during the times I wasn't otherwise occupied.

I started my practice in 2009, really small, just like most people do, as a solo operator. Of course, I made all the mistakes that I watch every bookkeeper make now, and it took me nearly half a decade before I worked my way through all those mistakes. So these days I call my first five years the 'f*ck-up' years.

But the great thing is, even when I was making mistakes – or maybe especially when I was, come to think of it – I was learning. Every single day I learned something new, and every single day I grew.

My Dad, who's one of Australia's most successful entrepreneurs, says that some people will work at a job for a year and every day they'll learn something new. So after a year, they have these 365 days of new and amazing experience, and their lives are richer for it. But some people can go and do the same thing every day for ten years, and at the end of that ten years they haven't learned anything at all. So even though they have ten years under their belt, they actually have less experience than the person with a year.

I don't know about you, but I never want to be that person, one who is essentially living the same day over and over again without growing in any way.

Right from the first day in my little practice, I worked hard to learn. And although there were plenty of f*ck ups in the f*ck up years, not a day went by that didn't contribute to my growth, the harvest of experience I was reaping, and the eventual success of my business.

In just five years, I had successfully built my thriving lifestyle practice to the point where I could choose my own adventure. And that's something I really want to pass on to you. I want my bookkeeping tribe to be able to choose their own adventure.

It's not for me to tell you what your adventure is – I hope you know that yourself, or that you'll discover it as we go on. But in my case, my first objective was to scale my business to the point where it could operate without me. In five years, I accomplished that mission. My little practice had become a solid business with a team of talented bookkeeping specialists, offering a range of services to clients, and eventually evolving into our big game. In the last year or so, we've reached the point where we're also able to give back through our commitment to *Free to Shine*, a child protection agency that helps keep young Cambodian girls from being trafficked into the commercial sex industry.

I ended up working what people kind of commonly call the four-hour work week, which meant that I could draw a nice income that allowed me to really enjoy myself and spend genuine quality time with my family – and take off on adventures when the opportunity arises.

Importantly, that also gave me the time to focus on my own health. So I was able to invest some real time into to prioritising my mental, spiritual and physical health, working on everything from diet to mindfulness, and that made a massive difference to my life. I became more effective, more energetic, and able to accomplish so much more.

And that in turn led to my next adventure, which has a working title of *The Healthy Bookkeeper.* It's a passion project I'm working on, and it will allow me to share my experiences in finding the healthy bookkeeper I always knew was inside me. Stay tuned for that one!

Now, that's enough about me for the time being. I hope this gives you some idea of why I do what I do and the way I do it, and why my experience will be of benefit to you.

The short version is that in the last dozen or so years, I haven't just been a bookkeeper really – I've become a sales and marketing expert with particular reference to marketing a bookkeeping business. I've become a dab hand at meeting with clients and the conversion process. And I've built powerful experience in the arts of creating and implementing bookkeeping systems, recruiting talented teams, and making the whole thing work together smoothly.

I'm sure that using my secret sauce method, you can do the same.

How to use this book.

I need you to do something for me, and that is to read this book all the way through before you begin to implement any of the practices I'll describe. It's essential that you get a broad understanding of the whole recipe before you start putting the ingredients together.

And if you come to a part where you think to yourself, "oh, hey, I already know this stuff," don't just skip it, okay? The rules of the game are that you should never think to yourself, "I know," because it stunts personal and professional growth. When someone is trying to teach me something, if I've heard it before, I approach it like I'm hearing it for the first time. If you do that, it will get you where you want to go easier.

Once you've digested the whole book end-to-end and you can see how each of my ingredients is connected and works with the others, you can go back and treat each chapter separately.

Each chapter provides you with details on how you can create your own secret sauce and make your transformation from bookkeeper to strategic bookkeeper, so I recommend that after that first 'global' read, you go back and deal with each element in order, thoroughly.

I've broken this book up into seven of the most important aspects of your business you'll need to adopt or sharpen up to become a thriving strategic bookkeeper, and they are:

- Your brand.
- Your menu.
- Client Attraction.
- Conversion.
- Succession.
- Your systems.
- Your team.

As you read and learn about these 7 principles, I think you'll find the first 5 the most earth shattering. Now, "earth shattering" might sound like a big claim - *but that is my intention* – to give you truly new thought leadership for a powerful transformation - becoming a strategic bookkeeper.

The last two are absolutely essential elements to get right, and I will give you some new ideas and techniques there.

As we go through these seven ingredients of my secret sauce, together we'll reshape your business so that your clients come to see the benefits you bring to them, and in the process become more loyal, appreciative advocates of your services.

That's the big goal – to turn your customers into your best advertisement. To make them not just loyal, but actual brand ambassadors, and to get them to help you expand your client list through their advocacy.

I know that you have the ability to carry off every step in my program, and I'm excited about the fact that when you do, there are big things in store for you. Remember, this is a book by a bookkeeper for bookkeepers – we share the same skills and the same love of numbers and systems, so I am super confident that we can do this together.

Let's go!

Chapter 2. Your Brand.

Remember when I said that my first five years were my "f*ck up" years? Not paying enough attention to my brand was one of my earliest and biggest f*ck ups.

When I started my practice, I said to myself, "Jeannie, you need a brand." So I went out and got myself a business name, a logo, website and some cards – not understanding that these are *brand assets*, not brand itself (more on that below).

"I don't need to think too much about my brand," I said to myself. "After all, I'm not Coca Cola, I'm a bookkeeper. People are going to hire me for my bookkeeping skills – they're going to choose me for what I can do and the benefits I can bring to their business rather than because they like my brand."

But the fact is, unless your market can connect with your brand (which is your *why*, not your *what*), you'll get lost in the crowd rather than stand out from it. To get people to look at what you can offer, how you go about it, what your clients say about you, what your systems and your team are like, your brand needs to appeal to your prospective clients from the first time they encounter it.

The beauty of having a strong brand is that it really does pull you out from the crowd, and it can help you avoid having to compete on price. You'll be selected on the basis of the success and value you project, rather than your hourly rate.

Becoming a brand isn't easy, but it's necessary.

Now, I get it. We're bookkeepers, and we don't want to be too flashy or put ourselves out there, we just want to offer our service to people who need it. And you know what? When I started, I thought the same.

To be honest, I had no real idea of what a brand really is, let alone how to construct one. I didn't understand the power of a brand to generate an idea of who you are and what you can do with just a few words, a look and a personality. I created my brand *assets* before nailing my *brand* – I focussed on the *what* and *how* when I should have been concentrating on the *why*.

It was only later that I realised how pivotal a powerful brand is to success.

Let's start with what a brand isn't.

Like so many people, I fell into the trap of thinking that a brand is just the assets that make it up – the logo, the website, business card, brochures, social media profiles.

Now, this is a key point, so I'm going to rinse and repeat a bit here, but it will be worth it. A lot of what we'll do in the coming chapters revolves around how I define "assets" in your Bookkeeping Practice. Because I'll be showing you how to create key assets in every discipline – brand assets, client attraction assets, conversion assets, SOP's and more. They're all a part of your IP*, and just like other assets you're familiar with (shares, property etc), powerful IP will provide you with great returns long after you build it.

**Intellectual property is another critical concept that we need to go into in greater depth, and we'll do that a bit later. Suffice to say that your collective IP is one of the reasons your clients will be loyal, your charges can be higher, and your brand can be more powerful.*

So, what is a brand?

In a nutshell, your brand is your organisation's "personality". Just as you have a personality, so does your organisation – and so does every successful organisation.

Just as you have hopes and dreams and values – and special people who "get you" – so should your organisation.

"Brand" is about eloquently conveying who you are, what you stand for and who you're compatible with.

And that's why "why" is at the heart of your brand. It's your *why* that will connect you with your market and build advocacy, because people will admire, identify and relate to your style, your vision, your goals and your character.

While travelling in Europe I came across this sign, and I think it sums up what a brand is really well.

That's me, in beautiful Malta, looking pretty good considering we were in the middle of a heat wave.

My "vibe" is my brand – The Strategic Bookkeeper.

Your vibe is your brand. It's your *why*, your *how* and your *what*. And your vibe, my friends, will attract your tribe – people who'll become advocates for you even before they become clients (I'll teach you how that works in later chapters).

Simon Sinek talks about the "why, how and what" in his book *Start with Why*, which I highly recommend. He provides examples of organisations who've succeeded or failed, and their connection, or lack thereof, to their *why*.

Take Apple for example.

Apple is a great example of an amazing brand.

The careful construction and management of the Apple brand has attracted a tribe of raving fan customers who are champing at the bit for the release of their new and updated products – and for which they're prepared to pay twice as much as they would for the same things from another brand.

When you think of Apple what do you think of? I think of cool design, hip users, awesome innovation and mind-blowing tech. Feelings I just don't get when I think of competing brands like HP, Del, Asus, Lenovo.

In *Start with Why* Simon Sinek points out that Apple was not the first tech organisation to release an MP3 player, but it was the most successful. Why? Because they started with why. People don't buy what you do/make, they buy why – Steve Jobs famously pitched the IPOD with the slogan: "1,000 songs in your pocket." Their product pitch started with why, not what. They nailed their brand and connected with their market in a way that others simply couldn't. That's the magnetic attraction of brand.

If you let me help you nail your brand, you will stand out from the crowd and reap the rewards over time as you play the long game and do your laps around the sun.

Brand makes everything easier.

When I first started, I didn't prioritise building my brand, because I thought there were higher value activities that would build my dream practice. And sure, there's lots to do. But what I didn't realise is that nailing your brand makes everything easier.

Your brand is like the concrete slab of your house. It will set you up with a foundation to create success – just like it did for Apple.

It's the gift that will keep on giving.

Once people know, like and trust your brand, they'll consider you to be the kind of bookkeeping service that they might want to do business with. So that first step – getting them to identify with your brand and entertain the idea that maybe, just maybe you're a good match for them, is absolutely indispensable to building the relationship.

Look around the world and think about the most successful brands. It's about personality, but it's more than that – it's about the substance behind it, the values they hold and the way they approach everything they do. There's a consistency that radiates through the whole organisation, from the colours and the typeface they use, to the way you're greeted at the front door.

That's what you need to build

As a solid foundation on which to build your success, your brand needs to have all the right ingredients in it. I'm talking about a powerful vision for what your practice will represent, a set of values and ethics that will guide everything you do and that you'll be proud to share with your potential clients, and an approach to communication and visual style that's unique and memorable and speaks your market's language. So right from the start it needs to reflect your ideals, your plans, your goals and your approach.

A trap for young players.

You may be tempted to reach out to a "marketing professional" for help in building your brand. I did, thinking that my investment would pay dividends. But – too late – I found out that "marketing" is a bit of a catch-all phrase that covers a wide range of different disciplines. Disciplines whose practitioners usually aren't expert in anything but their own field.

"Brand" is a discipline of marketing all on its own – a graphic designer is not a brand strategist, and a brand strategist is not a copywriter.

Now, the "marketing profession" is not licensed or regulated like bookkeeping is – so on top of there being a whole lot of very different marketing disciplines, anyone and their dog can "do marketing" for a living – which will be one discipline – and none of them will really help until you've done the hard work around formulating your brand.

When you're starting out in business, the last thing you need is to spend money on people and things that don't deliver the results you need, so it's really important that you don't fall into the same trap that I did.

Work through my *Brand Building Playbook* (link below) and build the intellectual property around your brand using the tools I provide.

Put your heart into it, and keep on developing your brand style, look, language and all the rest of it, until you've nailed it.

Then later you can use that IP to inform (brief) any marketing professionals you might be working with to build your *brand assets*. Don't do it the wrong way round by expecting the brand asset makers to make your brand – that's something you need to do yourself.

I have a brand expert on my team at *The Strategic Bookkeeper,* and he has a team too. Even he finds it hard to find marketing professionals who truly understand "brand" – so trust me now and believe me later... you are best off doing this work yourself (or you can subscribe to my tribe, and we'll do most of it for you).

How to make your brand "sing".

Remember when I said that "your vibe attracts your tribe". Your vibe is your vibe right? It can't be manufactured, it has to be honest. You can't pretend to be something you're not.

But to be clear, what we're talking about now is your organisation's "vibe" which is a little bit separate from you. Not totally separate, just separate in as much as it's connected to "the hat you wear at work".

We all wear many hats – the mum hat, the wife hat etc. I think this is a great concept to grasp. Because even though there's only one you, you adapt and change to suit each environment you're in – you regularly change which hat you're wearing. We all do it – consider the way you are with your best friend, your kids, and your clients – each of them sees a different side of you.

The business side of you is the seeds of your brand. When you step into your Bookkeeping Practice each day you wear the bookkeeper hat. And hopefully soon you'll wear the Strategic Bookkeeper hat.

So as you develop your brand I absolutely want you to be you – to paraphrase the amazing Dr Seuss:

"There has never been anyone You-er than You"

Creating your own Brand Playbook.

To guide you through building or renovating your brand, step by step, I've created the *Brand Building Playbook*. When you work through that, you'll end up with your own *Brand Playbook*, which will be incredibly useful to you.

There's a specific process I recommend you use to create your brand from the ground up, and it involves a lot of self-examination. If you've never engaged in this sort of inner enquiry before, it can be difficult to know where to start. But relax and enjoy the process, and don't be afraid to explore your motives, your ambition, and your feelings about it.

It's all about discovering your *why*, because when you understand that you'll be ready to work on the *how* and the *who*, which are of course also crucial to building your brand.

There's a bit of work to be done, and some of it might pull you outside your comfort zone. But, to rinse and repeat... success is in the long game. Read the book right through, then circle back and use the *Brand Building Playbook*. Step by step you're sure to get there.

If you join my program, then everything in the Brand Building Playbook will be provided as done-for-you assets. We'll show you how to edit and use them in your practice. You can find out more at: https://www.thestrategicbookkeeper.global/waitlist.

If you're DIY'ing then let's get stuck into it. You can download the Brand Building Playbook for free at https://www.thestrategicbookkeeper.global/bookresources[1] and work through the following steps.

Please note that I elaborate on all of these steps in the Brand Building Playbook.

Step 1 – what's your secret sauce?

Your secret sauce recipe already exists, you just haven't written it down yet. What's your process? What's your customers' journey from problem to solution? This is about getting clear yourself, so you can illustrate to your market "why" as well as how you can help. This will make you stand out from the crowd and give you a competitive advantage.

Step 2 – What problems do you solve?

Taking the time to workshop your market's problems is an exercise that Bookkeepers rarely engage in and yet, it's the foundation of why we're in business – to solve a problem.

[1]URL: https://thestrategicbookkeeper.s3.ap-southeast-2.amazonaws.co m/TSB+Brand+Building+Playbook.pdf

Let's play a game of Q & A – What do your clients want? This is a question I've enjoyed asking my team over the years because invariably the answer is, "their bookkeeping done". No, that's not what they want, that's what they expect – they want a thriving business, a thriving life etc.

If you don't truly understand what problems you're solving with your "what", which is your services, you will miss the mark in your sales and marketing and struggle to retain clients, long term.

Step 3 – what's your strategic foundation?

If your brand is the slab on which your business is built, the strategic foundation is the architecture. A genius mix of the practical and the visionary, your strategic foundation will be based quite heavily on two statements – your vision and your mission.

This is something that a lot of people seem to get wrong. Don't write down what you think looks good to other people, write down your truth. Make it something you're proud to stand by. Your strategic foundation should have a number of different components, which usually encompass:

- Your Vision
- Your Mission
- Your Values
- Your Target Market
- Your Big Game

Your Vision.

Once you understand your market's problems then you'll be more prepared to develop your vision statement which is "why" you exist. I know you exist to do their bookkeeping but why? Why do they need their bookkeeping done? What's the prize? Use the Brand building playbook to guide you through this further.

Your Mission.

Writing your mission statement is an exercise in "what" rather than "why". It tells your market exactly how you plan to achieve your vision, and it's a statement that you can test everything against, that you do.

When you bring on new employees you can point to your mission statement and say, "as part of my team, this is now your mission too.

Getting clear on your mission by using the Playbook will help you "speak to your market in language they can understand" to stimulate positive results – and it will help your team get clarity as well.

Your Values.

I've spent quite a lot of time developing and refining our team core values. From key words to key phrases that help us all live and breathe our vision and mission – while completing my laps around the sun.

When something's not working it's our values we look to first. Are we all living our values? If we're not, how can we support each other to step up?

Your core values have the power to underpin everything – including your standard operating procedures. Use the playbook to develop yours.

Your Target Market.

By now, you should be able to see your brand taking shape. You have an ethical framework in your values, and you understand the "why" and the "how" of your business.

Now is the time to think about *who* you want to work with – the clients who you would choose to work with, because working with them will be a delight rather than a drama.

It's also about what kind of people will relate to you and your brand – "the tribe that's attracted by your vibe."

Working through this section of my *Brand Building Playbook* will show you how to drill down to find your ideal clients.

Your Big Game.

In this final part of building your brand, I want you to think about your bigger purpose – how you come full circle to reconnect with the community (locally, globally) through your giving strategy.

In the *Playbook,* I talk about my Big Game, how my team and I give back, and what our dreams are in that direction. I hope that will inspire you to investigate ways that you can create your own "profit through purpose", because it's so rewarding a fulfilling to use your success to help others.

Okay, you're ready to build your brand.

I know, it's a bit hectic working through all the steps necessary to build your brand's strategic foundation, but I'm sure you'll agree that it's worth it. Thanks to my *Brand Building Playbook*, you now have all the pieces of the puzzle, and it's just a matter of putting them all together and seeing what your brand looks like.

And just to rinse and repeat here, if it all seems too daunting, you can join my program and we'll work through all the foundational issues with you, and then provide all the brand assets you need to kick off your branding journey.

But before we move onto the next bit, I'll just share a bit of my story with you, because I think there are some important lessons in it.

My branding journey.

Once I decided on my path to helping other bookkeepers, I decided to invest further in brand, knowing that the time and money spent, and the intellectual property that I've now spent years developing, would one day bear fruit for others.

My own bookkeeping practice was and has always been ground zero in terms of testing. I've put in the time and effort, not to mention a lot of money, to build, test, refine and improve my brand, so that you get the benefit of my experience.

It's been quite a journey, but I would do it all again because I think I've created something quite special for the bookkeeping community.

Meet Mickey.

One of the best decisions I've made was in engaging Mickey, a brand veteran.

Together we took my good foundation and made it great. We circled back on the Strategic Foundation and the Marketing Playbook I already had in place, and we dived in deeper to help my brand to connect more deeply with my market.

From the intensive work we did around brand, we ended up scrapping some assets and redoing them, updating others, and introducing new ones. Along the way we tested and measured everything on the stone of the market.

We evolved from bookkeepers to Strategic Bookkeepers. We evolved from Cloud 9 Book keeping to Cloud 9 Strategic, to meet the market and to solve their problems rather than serve up functions.

It took a few laps around the sun to get it all into the amazing shape it's in today, and our questioning, testing, refinement and improving continues to this day, to serve you.

Your brand playbook is now your marketing plan as well as your brand genealogy.

Once you are satisfied with your "perfect version 1" *Brand Playbook* (it doesn't actually have to be absolutely perfect because you can always improve it later – that's why it's Version 1), you can give to marketing professionals like graphic designers to create brand assets. Brand assets which, when developed off the back of a solid brand, will be far more likely to have the impact you intend them to have.

There are a lot of different assets you can choose from and the more common – because they're usually more effective – include:

- Website pages
- Social media profiles
- Social media posts

- How-to mini books and eBooks
- Blogs
- Videos
- Business cards
- Car wraps

There are thousands of other ways to get your message out there – marketing is after all "any activity that generates revenue" – so you need to be a bit discerning in what you spend your money on.

If you find an affordable brand expert (aka a unicorn) then I also recommend a brand style guide. If you join my tribe and you want Mickey to develop this for you, he has a proven effective process for this. Unfortunately, he doesn't have a never-ending capacity and so I'm unable to recommend him to anyone outside the tribe.

It's all about your "you-ness".

Before we wrap up the chapter on brand – and I hope you have a better understanding of how integral it is to everything that you do in your business – I just want to reiterate that your brand is all about you. It needs to be authentic, and that means it needs to reflect your goals and your approach.

You need to be the origin and the driver of your brand, and it must be true to who you are and what you aspire to be. There will always be people who don't get or simply don't choose your brand, and that's okay. You can't be all things to all people, and if you try you'll fail. So, as I like to say to my kids, "be yourself, because everyone else is taken."

One more thing...

When you become a strategic bookkeeper, that becomes a part of your brand – a part of who you are and how you do things. That means committing to doing things the strategic way, embracing the strategic approach and utilising the tools I've developed to build your business.

You're welcome to adapt the program to your own needs, and apply your own personality to everything. But for the sake of the bookkeeping community and industry we're creating – and for the sake of your clients – please deliver on your vision, your mission and your values in order to serve your tribe. If you do that, you can't go wrong.

Chapter 3. Your menu.

Your menu is one of the most important tools in your practice, because it's one of your first communications with your prospective clients. Where your brand is based on the *why* of your business, your menu is based on the *why* of the services you offer. It's about offering clients solutions.

Prelude – a note on my thought leadership.

Before we talk about the value of a menu, and then discuss my *Menu Playbook*, we need to have a quick look at some terms and language coming up in this and subsequent chapters. As you know, my thought leadership is built around some unique concepts and ideas, and I use a range of different words, acronyms and terms to convey my meaning. Here are just a couple that we'll use more often from here on in:

- *PC = Prospective Client.* They've touched your brand somehow – for example their accountant told them about you and now they're following you on social media. They're in your space, and ready to be convinced to join your tribe.

- *VIP = your actual clients*. You're in a relationship and you've invested in each other and are exchanging value. That makes them very important people!

Let's also rinse and repeat on the following:

- *Brand asset*. This term covers a wide range of assets, and in the case of your menu it's a digital brand asset – one that's very much a child of your brand. It's also a client attraction, conversion and succession asset – in fact, it's a systems and team asset too. And the one thing we know about assets is, they make us money. So they should – you work bloody hard to build them
- IP = Intellectual Property. IP can be a very misunderstood concept. Digital assets are IP in that they contain your ideas and the key to understanding your processes. Unlike time-for-money trading, you generate an element of IP once, then embody it in a digital or print asset, and then generate revenue from it forever (although you can always refine it down the track).

To help with all this, I've created a free resource for you – my *Menu Playbook*. You can download it here: https://www.thestrategicbookkeeper.global/bo okresources, and it will be a massive help to you in building your own menu.[2]

The difference between a menu and a price list.

Most bookkeepers present their proposals with their services and the price attached which means they lead with "what". A Strategic Bookkeeper presents their value with a menu which means they lead with "why".

You'll hear me bang on about "starting with why" throughout the book because it's a concept and a skill that will underpin your thriving practice.

Remember when I said, "*everything has the meaning we give it*". In terms of presenting your "*services and their attached price*", I'm going to call this your "*price list*", regardless of whether you're 'value' or 'fixed' pricing.

A pricelist is an essential tool, one you use

---

[2]URL: https://thestrategicbookkeeper.s 3.ap-southeast-2.amazonaws.com/TSB+Menu+Building+Playboo k.pdf

internally, to determine what mix of functions and features you'll be recommending to your clients, the anticipated cost of sales, gp and so on.

It's also the "*what*" part that I'll show you how to present at the right time in the conversion process, when you read that chapter next.

When I use the term menu, I don't want you to think of a restaurant but rather a day spa. Many moons ago I worked as a Beauty Therapist, and this is where I learnt the power of menu over price list.

Just like a beautiful day spa menu relaxes, your menu will actually relax your PC's and VIP's because it's designed to show them that you understand their problems and how you'll solve them.

Your clients first and foremost want you to demonstrate your authority and competence. You won't achieve this by leading with your price list but rather, your menu.

In fact, your menu will often articulate your PC's and VIP's problems in a way that they, themselves, can't. When this happens just watch their shoulders drop as they relax and feel like they've fallen into the hands of someone who understands them and can truly help them.

A menu is about showing your clients value and outcomes rather than your price. Which in turn makes them value and outcome focussed rather than cost focussed.

What is more appealing to you - the vehicle or the destination?

A really powerful concept I'd like you to grasp is that your services are like a *vehicle* that is used to drive to a wonderful *destination*.

When I bought a bicycle recently, it wasn't *really* the bike I was interested in, it was riding along the esplanade at Burleigh Heads on the Gold Coast. It was the sheer bliss I would feel when doing that. When I rave about my bike, I'm really raving about what it's doing for me and where it's taken me.

Your clients and your services are the same. Your PC's and VIP's need to see how your services will solve their problems, where they'll take them, and how they'll make them feel, in order to value you.

What is a menu?

At its simplest, a strategic bookkeeper's menu is a digital asset that conveys your value. It tells your PCs and clients *why* they need your services, because it eloquently conveys the problems you'll solve for them and how you'll solve them.

If we go back to the idea of a day spa, think about why customers book them. Because they're stressed, worn out, feeling in need of indulgence and relaxation.

It's the same with bookkeeping. When PC's reach out it's because they're confused, worried and under pressure. They feel like they're falling behind and they need help. They want a professional to take control, to reassure them that everything is going to be fine, and to prescribe exactly the right treatment.

That's what a good menu does.

When I go through my menu with PC's, I usually see the relief written all over their face when they realise they've come to the right place. I tell them our *why,* which is our Vision, our *how*, which is our Mission, and our *what*, which is in two parts.

But the big change comes when I show them my one page solution (OPS – which I'll explain fully below). And honestly, when we get to the final step of that OPS, which is the Payoff, again, their shoulders just drop. They relax. The price becomes secondary, and they're happy to pay whatever the cost.

Our goal is to help them realise that strategic bookkeeping doesn't cost money, it makes money while it provides peace of mind. And when they get that, they're beaming. Often the first thing they do is go off and rave about it to their friends. That's part of the appeal of strategic bookkeeping.

Why you need a menu.

The goal is to create a menu as a key digital asset to use in your business. One that will help you show your clients your value and in turn, will make them value you.

We already know that you're a highly skilled, experienced bookkeeper capable of delivering excellent standards of work – but how do you get your PC's and VIP's to see this? How do you get them to understand the value you're adding not just to their business but their lives? With a menu.

As you guide your client through your menu, you're helping them to see that Strategic Bookkeeping is one of the major keys to a healthy, thriving business – which is ultimately what they want. You build their trust in you because you're able to clarify their problems and describe your solutions. At each step they become more aware of the issues you're describing and more willing to take that next step and start a relationship with you.

I have met so many class A bookkeepers who, despite their skills and record, have been unable to find clients who value them. Too many of us end up getting stuck with cost-focussed clients telling us how to suck eggs. And that's soul-destroying.

It's also why menu is your second most important asset (after brand).

All it takes is a simple shift.

The smallest shift in the way you do things can make an enormous difference.

Let me tell you a story. When my gorgeous special needs child Rory was four, we went to a clinic because I could see that we both needed support. And that was a really low point for me, because my perception was that I was failing as a parent. I couldn't get the parenting outcomes I desired, so I must be doing it wrong, right?

Well as it turns out the wonderfully professional people at the clinic helped me to see that in the main, I was already doing all the right things, but in some ways, I wasn't communicating what I wanted Rory to do in ways he could respond.

For example, rather than endlessly telling the kids my rules, they got me to write them all up on a big sheet of butchers' paper and hang them on the wall. Everybody knew what the rules were, they agreed to them, and hey presto, massive improvement.

A few little shifts like that made all the difference.

You're already a great bookkeeper, right! Please don't doubt yourself like I did as a parent, and never let anyone tell you that if you can't find and keep clients, you're not a grade A bookkeeper.

If you're having trouble in that area, I would suggest it likely has nothing to do with your skills as a bookkeeper, it's more that you're not aware of the principles in this book. Which is why I'm here – to teach you and help you apply those powerful lessons.

Productising your services.

One of the biggest and most beneficial changes you can make to your practice and your life is to stop pricing what you do in terms of the time it takes and start pricing according to the value and outcomes you deliver to your clients.

"Give a man a fish and he'll eat for a day. Teach him to fish and he'll never go hungry," goes the old proverb. I want to give you great principles and teach you to "fish", to learn how to productise your services.

It's all about packaging a number of services into a value bundle – as I'm sure you know phone and internet companies, and many others do. Putting *products* rather than *services* on your menu is critical to its success, and to communicating the value you build into everything you do.

There's a list of ways you can productise your services in the *Menu Playbook*, so please make use of it. There's also more on productising in *Chapter 4 – the Power of Client Attraction*.

Let's rinse and repeat for a minute.

In the last chapter on Brand, we developed your organisation's personality, and learned the difference between a brand and a brand asset.

You can see now that your menu is a potentially powerful brand asset, which you'll primarily use in attraction, conversion and succession (which we'll talk about in the next few chapters). But your menu is also a systems and team asset, because you and your team must first be clear around your menu before you're able to convey it eloquently to your PC's and VIP's.

What a menu does.

It starts with *why* so that your clients begin with the end in mind. It explains how you'll get there. It clarifies the problems and the payoffs, and it illustrates the steps involved in solving the problems.

It makes your *what* (which is your services)

make sense, and in doing so, it gives everyone a framework to build the relationship on.

Without further ado, let's get to work on your menu.

I'm just going to give you an outline of how to create a menu here – but for a practical, step by step guide to how to create a menu, because there are more detailed instructions in my *Menu Playbook*.

You can download it here: https://www.thestrategicbookkeeper.global/bookresources, if you didn't download it already.[3]

If this is your first lap around the sun, it's probably easier to keep your menu as simple as possible because you can always refine and expand it later. I use a single page menu because it's simple, direct and persuasive.

To rinse and repeat: Don't get caught up trying to develop version 2 before version 1. Whatever you come up with will be your perfect version 1.

Step 1 – Your why and your how.

---

[3]URL: https://thestrategicbookkeeper.s3.ap-southeast-2.amazonaws.co m/TSB+Menu+Building+Playbook.pdf

You've already completed this step on the way to developing your brand – your *why* and your *how* are your Vision and Mission statements. It's important to put these on your menu, but (and this is where you'll need the help of a graphic designer who understands emphasis and balance) they need to take a bit of a back seat to the next step.

Step 2 – Your "one page solution".

Your one page solution (or OPS) is where you present your PC (or VIP as you'll see in succession) with the solutions to the problems that are besetting them, and win them over to your way. It's a digital asset that you can email, message, print, or include in presentations – a quick, easy read that takes the PC on a fast journey from pain to relief.

Illustrating the problems.

As mentioned, when a PC comes to you, they're almost certain to be confused about and struggling with something or other, and the moment you prove to them that you appreciate what's troubling them, you'll have their confidence.

So the first thing to do is to recognise and describe the problems that they are struggling with most.

You know as well as I do, the kind of problems that beset small business owners, so list 3 to 5 of them. Make the descriptions short and to the point.

When you demonstrate that you understand their problems more eloquently than your PC's do, it builds you as an authority – which naturally leads them to trust that you can solve those problems.

Provide steps to solving their problems.

The next step is to create a guide as to how you will work together to solve the problems they're suffering. I use a 4-step process from problem to solution, but you might have other ideas.

The goal is to prescribe the solution and explain what a return to a healthy business looks like.

The Payoff.

It's crucial that your menu describes the ultimate payoffs which is another word for solutions. If you have 3-5 problems, what are the 3-5 payoffs? If a problem is stress, perhaps a payoff is peace of mind and so on. This is about showing your PC or VIP where the journey will take them – if they go on the journey with you.

Step 3 – The call to action.

You'll notice that your one page solution and your menu don't include a description of your services. That's intentional.

The first reason I do it that way is that your PC or VIP will be much more interested in your personal recommendations for what you can do for them, than trying to figure out from a services list what they need.

The second is that your menu can simply include a call to action to visit your website if they want to see the services list. Getting a PC to visit your website to gain a greater appreciation of your brand is always a good idea, so any excuse you can make to get them there is a good one.

Step 4 – Brief a creative on your menu design.

Abraham Lincoln once said, "Give me six hours to cut down a tree and I'll spend the first four hours sharpening the axe." I love that because it speaks to the power of preparation. So when you brief a designer or creative on putting your menu together as a digital asset, you need to give them the sharpest possible axe.

In other words, give them your full brand story, ensure that they understand your *why* and your *what* as well as your *how*, talk to them about your target markets, and share your Big Game. The more familiar your creatives are with your brand, its personality, goals and methods, the more attuned to your brand values the menu they create for you will be.

Allow for three rounds of edits in your budget, and voila, your menu is created.

It's a great day for a daydream.

Remember I said you ought to read this whole book through before you take any of the actions I recommend. But don't let that stop you from letting the ideas surrounding your menu percolate in the back of your mind as you go on.

Let your mind wander – daydream with pen and paper, sitting somewhere nice (I do it while looking out at Burleigh Mountain from my Gold Coast home).

A terrific resource here is the book *Will it make the boat go faster?* by Olympic gold medal rower Ben Hunt-Davis and executive coach Harriet Beveridge. If you're like me, you'll get the

Blinkist app to distill the book's message into a short 15 minute reading or listening bursts.

Some things to daydream about.

As I said above, you need to get through this whole book, then work through your branding before you can get to creating a menu. But in those times when you are letting your mind wander around your menu, think about things like this:

- What services do you offer right now? How do they solve problems?
- What is the logical order in which clients "pick up" your services? Do they tend to need catch up work first? Is there something they need even before catch up work is done, like a file audit?
- What's your process in diagnosing and dealing with your clients' problems? Where do you start? Where *should* you start? Are the two the same?
- If you're not yet offering services which illuminate the numbers (the way you will do when you become a strategic bookkeeper) where would you start?

Just daydream, just scribble. It's fun and it's helpful – and you may be surprised how one little spark can start a fire.

Never set and forget.

As I've done my laps around the sun as a Bookkeeper in Practice I've continued to innovate around product and pricing, year on year - which includes our menu.

In one year, a few years ago, after really digging into price and product innovation (just like I'm asking you to) we doubled our profits. That's the real power of menu, of starting with *why*, of doing the sometimes-frustrating work of retraining our bookkeeper brains to move from a world where we sell features and functions to one where we sell value and outcomes – where we talk problems and payoffs.

So the takeaway here is, always keep daydreaming about your brand and your brand assets, because you can always find ways to improve them. And if you're like me, you'll enjoy the process of letting your mind take you where it will.

A note on your services.

We started this chapter with an examination of why a menu is different from a price list (which is really a services list), and why you should utilise your menu much more frequently and effectively than a price list.

We noted that your PC's and VIP's will always prefer your personalised recommendations over your list of services. But you will of course need a services list, which can be accessed on your website and used to help you put together proposals.

Now, I won't go on about this too much because it's not a major part of my system, but there are a few things I can help you with in regard to your services.

As with your menu, it pays to keep refining and improving the range and detail of your services as you keep making laps around the sun. It will help you understand what problems you solve, and it will make your *why* become clearer, so your copy will get sharper, and it will be easier to turn a PC into a VIP.

Service lists have another important function.

Your service lists also feeds directly into your Service Level Agreements (SLA's). They provide the detail around *what* you're promising to do, and form the basis of your SLA deliverables to your VIP's. So it's crucial that they are detailed, clear and concise. But here's the thing. Many bookkeepers lead with the detail (the *what*) – the service list – rather than the *why* – the menu.

How I can help.

If you join The Strategic Bookkeeper Transformation Program then everything in the Menu Building Playbook will be provided as done-for-you assets - properly branded, carefully worded over many iterations, and simple for you to implement.

As with every aspect of the information you'll find in this book, it's all my own work – I've created my entire system from the ground up, and I know it intimately. I've invested hundreds of thousands of dollars getting all my brand assets to the point where I can proudly say they're well designed, well written, and above all highly effective.

Something I'm really passionate about is "community". I truly believe it does take a village – to raise each other up. Which is why, as part of my program I put us all in "the tribe" – an online community where we come together, to follow the same method, to learn from each other and to grow together. You can find out more here: https://www.thestrategicbookkeeper.global/wa itlist.

Rinse and Repeat time.

We're almost ready to move on to the next chapter on *Attraction*, but before we do let's just rinse and repeat what we've learned in this chapter.

Your menu is one of the tools you'll need to build your brand, and it's all about how you'll move clients from problems to payoff. You need to demonstrate empathy with your PC's by talking about the kind of problems they're suffering, and how you'll fix them.

In other words, you need to start with your *why* – and show that you can appreciate the PC's *why* as well. Once you've established that, you can move onto the *what* and the *how* – but don't rely on these two elements to be persuasive. Your PC's and VIP's will be looking for your personal recommendations, not your service lists.

Use my *Menu Playbook* to create your menu, but don't try and over-achieve with your first draft. You can always come back to it later. Or better yet, join my tribe and take advantage of all the work I've done over years, by getting a done-for-you menu along with all the other brand help and brand assets my tribe members enjoy.

I'm excited, are you?

I do get excited. My clients have often laughed at just how excited I get when they're winning, and I'd love for you to experience and share that kind of excitement.

Becoming a Strategic Bookkeeper takes you, your clients, your business and your life to a whole new level. And creating your menu is a massive step in that direction. I hope you're as excited as I am at what becoming a Strategic Bookkeeper could mean to your future.

For some of you, the next section, on *Client Attraction*, will be one of the most important in this book. It deals with how you're going to attract clients to your business, so it's a deep dive into the art and science of marketing.

In subsequent chapters we'll deal with the ways that you'll convert those clients and then continue the journey with your succession services, which will delight them even more, and build your thriving practice through advocacy for your brand.

Chapter 4. The Power of Client Attraction.

Okay. Your brand and your menu are established, so you now have a growing resource of brand assets. In this chapter, we're going to look at building more brand assets, and how to put them to use in finding and attracting new clients.

I could quite easily (and happily) write a whole book on the subject of attraction, and one day I just might. But *Becoming a Strategic Bookkeeper* is about giving you the whole story around building your Strategic Bookkeeping Practice, so we kind of need to treat all of these pieces of the puzzle in a general, fundamental way. It's about getting you familiar with the concepts and principles involved, and notching up a few quick wins.

As this is your first lap around the sun, there's a lot to do and learn in this space, but as always, I encourage you to keep learning and improving with every "lap", because this is the long game and I want you to succeed at it.

More resources.

I truly hope that you'll become as fascinated and involved in the power of attraction as I am. And if you do, I'd love to welcome you as a listener and subscriber to my podcast, where we continue to dive deeper and deeper into the art and science of client attraction. It's a great place to continue to develop your skills in this crucial area.

While we're here, I'd also love to see you become a member of *The Strategic Bookkeeper's Way,* which is my community on Facebook. There we talk about attraction and its close cousin, succession which, as you'll learn in the next chapter, is all about transforming your practice beyond the bounds of finding new clients.

Now, before we begin...

Attraction is one of the hardest concepts for bookkeepers like you and me to become familiar with and to implement to our advantage. As you read on, you might get the urge to put this book down because we're getting into stuff that makes you feel uncomfortable.

All I ask is that you read the whole book before making judgements around what you think you can and can't do.

Redefine your expectations of yourself – make your current ceiling your new floor.

Open yourself to the possibility that actually, you *are* built for this – because I know you are. And if you read the book right through, you'll learn how right I am.

I promise, even though we'll be talking about things like marketing and even selling, attraction is more about being a "solver" than a "seller". So don't let the words and phrases make you shut down.

The only thing that stands between you and everything you ever wanted could be finishing this book. So "feel the fear and do it anyway".

As Dory said... just keep swimming... and she found Nemo. So just keep swimming – and let me help you find your thriving practice as a Strategic Bookkeeper.

A note on terminology.

Bookkeepers talk in terms of services, so I know you like to be clear about all the language used. So when I talk in terms of products, it's because services become products when they move them from being single items (like bookkeeping for $90 per hour) to being a bundle of items where we price the outcome – and we give that "product" a name. For example, a "Strategic Bookkeeping Package" is actually a package of individual services bundled together.

We'll talk more about this below in the section on productising your services, which we touched on in the last chapter.

Let's get some Attraction going!

Attraction is one of those concepts that makes a lot of bookkeepers just kind of freak out. The part where we talk about how to attract new customers to your business, which I know makes a lot of you cringe. Later we'll talk about conversion and succession, which are the flow-ons from attraction, so you need to get this part right before we move on. So please persevere with this chapter.

I have a special love for the process of client attraction, and I love the way it works. But I wasn't born this way. I had to work and learn the same as you. However, because of my family's business background I was never intimidated or scared of things like attraction and marketing. I had high expectations of myself in this area, and I met them.

Just remember, you can never exceed your own expectations, so going into this I want you to have high expectations that you'll succeed. I have confidence in you, so you should have confidence in yourself.

Okay let's use the S and M words.

Attraction is really just my way of saying sales and marketing. But don't worry, it won't hurt. In fact, I think it will make you feel better, because the bottom line is, I'm going to show you how to do sales and marketing with an absolute minimum of what you probably think of as sales and marketing. It's all about systems, which we bookkeepers love.

You're not alone.

Most bookkeepers struggle with this area. It's just a given. We're far more comfortable with being a great technician than we are singing for our supper – which is how a lot of people see "client attraction".

Globally, there are two – count 'em – two absolute top-level problems for bookkeepers. The first one, which will not surprise you, is getting paperwork out of clients. But the second is sales and marketing. It's something that affects us all, and those of us who are successful have succeeded because we've learned how to deal with it.

You can do it the hard way, which is to go it alone, as I did. Or you can do it the easy way, which is to benefit from my experience (as you are doing by reading this book).

I've invested well over a decade, and a lot financially, over that time in testing, measuring, refining and ultimately documenting my secret sauce method, which you can now learn and apply in your business.

Client attraction is an investment.

It's true, client attraction will cost you both time and money. You'll need to invest in brand assets, put time into learning the skills of attraction, and then put them to use.

But the good news is, if you invest your money and your time wisely, like any good investment it will bear dividends.

Your time investment.

Time is the first thing that you need to "spend" in order to gain the attraction skills that you need. Your investment in this area should include:

- Time to read this book and listen to my podcast.
- Time to implement what you learn.
- Time to do the high value activities that influence client attraction – which I'll teach you now.
- Time to keep developing and improving your skills, because the better you get, the more your practice will succeed.

Probably the best part of your time investment at this stage is that you only need to make a lot of your initial investment once. You'll get better at and more comfortable with attraction with every lap around the sun, and you'll end up with more free time to chase your own dreams.

Your financial investment.

Every business has set up costs and building your Strategic Bookkeeping Practice attraction arsenal is no different. You'll need to invest in brand assets like a logo, your menu, business cards, email signatures, email marketing, and so much more.

I recommend setting aside 5% of your annual revenue for marketing B2B (business to business). Also plan on spending 5% per annum on your own education and development. The figures I've quoted here are about average for most successful practices.

If you are thinking about joining my program, then your investment will be in marketing and in your education.

I've priced our program so that it's ridiculously accessible to every bookkeeper – bringing on just one new client and upgrading one client into your succession services will pay for it.

Are you five years old?

The five-year mark is where things change for a lot of business owners. There are statistics showing that growth is a bit of a curve. At five years you should have met a lot of people along the way, you probably have a thriving practice with pleased clients, and you should be able to live your dream on your terms. If you're five years or more in and you haven't achieved that, that's okay too. It just means you're still probably standing on a mountain of value that you don't know. I can really help you a lot there.

If you're less than 5 years old then you'll have fewer people in your network and so you may need to pay more attention to building that up. Don't worry, we'll be looking at strategies that will help you do just that.

Some client attraction concepts and tools.

As I hope you're beginning to understand, my thought leadership is a big part of my success. And sharing the principles and approaches I've refined over years means you can benefit from my thought leadership.

So let's jump into a couple of concepts and tools that I use in developing and implementing my attraction strategies. Later we'll talk about specific strategies and tactics, but for now it's about developing your understanding of my Strategic Bookkeeping way.

Farming versus hunting.

I often talk about attraction strategies as hunting or farming.

Hunting is an exercise in "catch and kill". It's also the "one at a time" approach. You go out, you "hustle" (work your butt off to convince them to try you) and you win *one* client.

For me, the best attraction strategies are about farming – and I believe that bookkeepers are farmers. "Farming" is about investing in fertile ground (your brand and brand assets, and your attraction strategies), planting your seed-crop, watering those seeds and then letting them grow and mature into a blooming harvest.

My "float" theory.

Attraction strategies are about bringing people into what I call your brand atmosphere, or *brandsphere*. The idea is that they float into your brandsphere – nine times out of ten they float in through your digital brand assets, which is why your brand and brand assets (in that order) are such critical drivers here.

The *why* is that people will float in because they have a problem they need help solving – and you're in the problem solving game (we all are).

The *how* is that whether they hear about you via a friend or some other network, or find you on google or whatever, they will float into your brand by engaging in one of your brand assets, most likely your website and social media.

The *what* is that people who float in won't always reach out to you there and then – most of the time they'll want to get to know you online until they're ready to reach out.

That may be when the pain of the problem is not big enough yet, they feel they really *know, like* and *trust* you, or they're ready to stop blaming time and money for not seeking help.

The point is that some people who float into your *brandsphere* will buy soon, some will buy later. Some won't buy at all, but they'll tell all their friends and family how fabulous you are. That's the power of building advocacy with your market, not just your clients.

The good news is, once they're in your *brandsphere*, you have their attention and you can engage with them, provide them with value, and communicate with them via the platform that suits them.

This is one very successful way that bookkeeping practices end up with a steady stream of enquiries which feeds them continuously – it's farming rather than hunting.

The amazing thing about having your brand on point is you're generally going to attract more of the right people, because everything you do is designed to attract your tribe and your people.

The power of advocacy.

In my system of attraction, there are three types of attraction strategies:

- Brand
- Advocacy
- Paid advertising

We can safely say that you understand the power of brand, and we'll talk some more about paid advertising later. The middle category, advocacy, is our next item on the list and it's one of my favourite aspects of the game.

Why? Because it involves helping people, and people helping you. It's a big roundabout of helping and being helped, and it works for everyone.

The advocacy marketing approach in a nutshell.

Advocacy marketing is an overarching term that applies to word of mouth, business networking, referral and so on – because it's the principle of advocacy that make these other forms of marketing actually work for you.

And that principle is: "If I provide you with value in order to help you do better in business, then you'll advocate for my brand, and eventually you may also do business with me."

Write it down. Put it on your office wall. Learn it. Live it.

And the great news is, you're built for it.

Do you love helping people? Of course! You're a bookkeeper. Can you follow a system? Yes. And as I told you, I built this system for bookkeepers.

Now you may be wondering *"how do I give someone value or create advocacy before they're even a client?"* which I promise I'll show you if you read on.

The benefits of advocacy marketing.

When someone is your advocate, they are out there actively telling others how you have helped them, drawing them into your *brandsphere.*

Once you've proven your value by helping them, why would they recommend anyone else? They'll buy when they're ready – and in the meantime they're out there telling people what a star you are. It's a win win situation.

And the beauty of the advocacy marketing approach is that it's a "slow burn" rather than a torrent of new clients you can't handle.

Later when we talk about strategies, I'll introduce my *Evergreen Advocacy Partnerships* agreement, which gives you a really easy structure for advocacy marketing, so it's important that you understand what it is.

Rinse and repeat time: advocacy marketing is about giving your market, your PC's (prospective clients) and your VIP's (clients) value – so that they become advocates of your brand – in a myriad of different ways which I'll show you as we progress further in this chapter.

Word of mouth marketing.

Word of mouth marketing is the result of using my overall secret sauce recipe. It's a powerful attractor that grows over time, and it's based on the value you build into your relationships and your practice. The only way to build word of mouth is over time – there is no silver bullet. Look for progress and build on it.

Productising your services.

This is a concept we first mentioned in the *Menu* chapter, but we'll refer to it again and again, so I just want to rinse and repeat on it. It also relates to how you can stop charging by the hour and get away from the trap of selling time and giving away your IP.

Also known as value bundling and several other names, productising confuses many bookkeepers. Ultimately, for a bookkeeper, it's taking all the services you provide yearly, quarterly, monthly or weekly, and bundling them all up into a monthly "product" for one flat fee. Don't price this product on the time it takes, price it on the value it delivers to the VIP. Give it a name and you've now "productised" that bundle of services.

A lot of businesses like telecommunications and internet providers, accountants and others use value bundling, so I'm sure you're aware of it.

When you productise or value bundle, your clients will see and feel your value, and it will help them stop stressing over next month's bill. You'll create recurring revenue, predictable cash flow, more efficient systems and higher profit margins.

Let's talk about brand assets.

A lot of my attraction strategies revolve around the use of brand assets like your website, database social media and so on, so you'll need to create or update these as part of your transformation to becoming a Strategic Bookkeeper in Practice.

You'll find a lot more detail and instruction around this in my *Attraction Playbook,* which is free to download here: https://www.thestrategicbookkeeper.global/bo okresources.[4]

If you're wondering how much of this is done-for-you in the program you'll find details at the end of this chapter, so skip ahead if you're super curious about that.

[4]URL: https://thestrategicbookkeeper.s3.ap-southeast-2.amazonaws.co m/TSB+Attraction+Playbook.pdf

Your profile.

One of the first things we look at in my *Attraction Playbook* is your profile, because it's so important.

"Profile" is a bit of an old school marketing principle, in that it used to relate to "public" figures. We're all public figures now, because we're all online. So it's become easier and more important for the average business "Jo" (that's you) to leverage profile as a client attraction strategy.

The more compelling your profile is, the more credibility you will have and the faster you'll build trust in your market. It gives PC's a reason to choose you over your competitors without cost as their first priority, because it demonstrates your value. And that means you can charge more.

Display your profile whenever and however you can as a digital asset and make it part of your vibe. Include your profile in all your important assets:

- Your website pages
- Your social media
- Your email signature

What to include.

Your profile is the place to present and verify your prowess as a business professional and as a bookkeeper, so it needs to include anything that furthers that aim, including:

- Software Company Badges & certifications
- Technical qualifications
- Formal registrations
- Licences and insurances
- Experience and expertise
- Awards
- Speaker or author
- Any additional recognised skills and experience

I'm guessing you probably have 5 out of that 8, but if not, that's ok. As you do more laps around the sun, you'll gain more.

In the next chapter we'll talk about how to include profile in your conversion process (along with other principals you've learned in this chapter), so when it's time (after you've read this book at least once), download my *Attraction Playbook* and use it to help you build your perfect profile.

About us.

In 2022 my marketing manager told me that our *About Us* page is our most visited website page. PC's go there and read about our prowess – our skills, experience, accolades and so on, and it obviously helps.

In 2021 I won 2 finalist positions, one with Xero, one with WIFA (women in finance) – I received media packs and badges which I could proudly display in my digital assets including my email signature.

In my program my team and I help and support the tribe to do the same – become finalists (which are an award with a media pack) and winners too.

Things like that re*ally boost my profile and help to make me the clear choice over my peers. The same will work for you too.*

Here's an idea.

If (when) you win an award, why not share the celebration with your network of accountants - even if that network is only one accountant -

this will build credibility with these valuable partners. And with your friends on social media - with a simple, informal post – when I did that, 136 people celebrated with me and several asked "Jeannie do you have room for a new client?"

Your website.

I'm sure you know that your website is an important digital asset, and it really must be kept up to date and relevant.

Now, you might think this means you need to get onto it first, but a website is something that definitely should not be rushed. When I rebranded, we updated our website last, and it just fell together with ease. We already had our *why*, our *what* and our *how* sorted, we had our brand and our menu in place, and we knew who we wanted to target. And because we had all those ducks in a row, it was easy to brief the web designer, and watch it all fall into place.

If you already have a website, wait until after you build your brand, your menu and your social media before updating it. My *Attraction Playbook* will be a big help in planning your website renovation, because I've listed the landing pages I recommend you include.

Websites and the internet change fast and need constant care, so for more information, listen to my podcast, follow and join my socials and subscribe to my email list for the ongoing advice we provide.

If you are part of The Strategic Bookkeeper program, we provide you with "done for you" web pages so you can put them straight into your existing website and hit the ground running, and we constantly update and improve the resources we provide, including web pages. Joining us helps you get to work fast and score some quick wins, and settle in to play the long game after that.

Your database.

Marketing is all about communication, and you want to communicate your message to the widest audience possible. That means gathering, maintaining, occasionally cleaning, and most important of all, *using* your database.

The first thing I want to look at with your database is the people that you know personally, and the rule here is, don't keep yourself a secret from family and friends. You need to tell everyone about yourself.

Starting your database.

My *Attraction Playbook* gives you pointers on building your database – another reason to download it. But you have to be careful about who you add to your database, and how you contact them, because there are rules in play.

There are potentially hundreds or even thousands of people who *could* be on your database – even if you have only one client, presumably they have an accountant, and that accountant could potentially be on your database. It's just a matter of learning how to connect with them and gaining their permission for ongoing contact. We'll talk more about that later in the KIT marketing section, and even more later in the *Succession* chapter.

Harvesting the diamonds at your feet.

One way to build your database is to pick up the "diamonds at your feet". And to illustrate how that works, I want you to think about an event.

Imagine that you run an event called "How to Fix your Cash Flow Woes" to attract PC's. You promote the heck out of it on social media – which you do really well because you've tuned into my podcasts on how to successfully mine social media markets – and 50 people register for the event. Perfect.

But then none of those 50 turn up. Failure, right? Wrong.

You have just created a database of 50 people who've admitted that they are struggling with cash flow! Now, you know and I know that a lot of small business owners don't really know what cash flow is and so most of them are just struggling, period. That's probably why they signed up for your event.

But regardless of their motivation, you now have fifty diamonds at your feet – people you can contact and communicate with them about how Strategic Bookkeeping is the solution – because you already have their permission to contact them at least once more, about their no show at the event.

I'll expand on how to make them into PC's later, but for now the point is, this is a great way to build your network and your database.

By the way...

As part of The Strategic Bookkeeper program, one of the things we give our tribe members as a "done for you" welcome line is an eBook. Called *The 7 Deadly Cash Flow Sins*, we can help you market the book as something you've co-authored, and we'll also teach you how to run it as a workshop.

That's just one of the assets we provide, that helps you build your database. And our program has assets for every step of my secret sauce.

Business networking.

Business networking is going to play a role in gathering names for your database. I know what you're thinking: "Yuk". Business networking can be icky, but it's also a good way to get to know people. It's a great way to just meet people, shake their hand and begin to build your know/like/trust rapport.

It's definitely not a place to collect business cards and put them on your database unsolicited – that's called spamming and that will only damage your brand. And you don't want to just get out there and indiscriminately throw business cards at people either, because you could attract all sorts of people you don't want.

It's a place where you talk to people about their businesses and their lives, and you seek to understand. Most important of all, a business network event is your opportunity to *find ways to give people value.* Listen to what they're saying with one question in your mind: *How can I help this person?* If you do that, you'll be able to offer them value, and they will be attracted to you and thank you for it.

A short digression into social media.

One last thing before we get into some powerful strategies around attraction. It relates to your digital brand assets such as your website and menu, but it also influences the way you execute the strategies and tools I am about to give you.

I want to talk about how you engage with your database, which, to be honest, is really simple.

When you talk to your friends and family, you phone, you email them, you text them, you send them something in the actual mail. You might

Zoom them, engage on social media and you also message on socials too, right? We live in a digital media age, which has been turbo-charged by the pandemic.

And that means your market wants to get to know you digitally – to see if they like you, to verify that you're trustworthy, and just to see if your vibe is their vibe. And they can do that 24/7 without you needing to be there, through social media.

That means your social media is working for you even when you're out living your dreams – and you can share new posts, ideas, thoughts and strategies from anywhere in the world. That's what I call extending your reach!

Know. Like. Trust.

You may already have heard of "know, like and trust" which are the three keys to turning a PC into a VIP. Where once we all had to do that face to face, now we can do it digitally.

Here's a fun fact. Our brains don't distinguish between digital and real in a lot of ways. So when people see you online, they develop a relationship with you digitally in a similar way to knowing you in person. That's why celebrity endorsements work – and why people think they "know" celebrities and get so attached to them.

And to get people to know, like and trust you, you give them value. You share your IP with them, give them some knowledge or advice for free - which I show you how to do in this chapter.

The "value approach".

In content marketing, which is pretty much what all social media is, don't ask yourself whether anyone will like it or not, only how valuable it is.

When I started out doing my own podcasts and appearing as a guest on other peoples' podcasts, I was terrified. But when I learnt to apply the "value approach", my nerves calmed. I was able to say to myself, "this isn't about me, it's about giving my audience (your clients) value in order to actually do better in business."

Even an inspirational social media post designed to boost one's mood can help someone do better in business.

The "value tool" is a great way to shape what you say every time you have to talk about yourself or your business, whether that's in your content marketing, your proposals, directly to a PC or VIP, or in a networking situation.

My social media.

At the time of writing this book, my preferential social media platforms are Facebook, Instagram, LinkedIn and YouTube, and I find that they're all great tools. But I have never become a slave to social media, and neither should you.

As with any other brand asset, any time you implement a social media strategy you need to measure and test your ROI (return for time and/or money).

A couple of attraction assets.

There are a couple of brand assets that we haven't covered yet, but which are crucial to your attraction strategies, so let's introduce them here. They are your product ladder and your lead (or welcome) lines.

Your product ladder.

A simple example of a product ladder is the local gym, where they offer a free or low-cost trial. You've floated into their brandsphere (online or by driving past), you have a problem that going to the gym could address and now, you can try before you buy with little or no financial risk.

You already have your core services, which is one part of your product ladder. But the first 2 steps on the ladder are your *general content* and *lead lines* which I also call welcome lines because they are designed to welcome PC's to try you in a low cost or no cost way.

Your content is a product because it's aimed at helping your market do better in business. Your core products are a natural part of your product ladder, of course. And when we get into *Succession* we'll look at further additions to your product ladder. Essentially, I'll lead you through a series of products (not services) that you can take your VIP's through, so that at every step up they get more value and knowledge.

But for now, the first step on the product ladder, lead lines – or as I call them, welcome lines.

Your welcome lines.

In the retail world, a lead-line is a low-cost product in a category that you covet, that leads you into a store to buy. But rather than buying that you upgrade a better model.

Let me tell you a very short story to illustrate. I decided I'd buy myself a cruiser bike, a good one. I did my research online and eventually found a reputable bike store with quality cruisers that seemed like amazing value.

I went into the store and told the assistant the bike I was looking for, and he showed it to me. Then, using the *value approach,* he told me about a bike that was twice as expensive but was, he assured me, ten times as good.

I took her for a spin, and I could see her value – I bought her and named her Summer. And Summer and I have been living happily together ever since, cruising on the path along the beach, riding along for hours in bliss.

The *lead line* combined with the *value approach* helped me do better in life – just like you can and will help people do better in business.

<u>How to develop your welcome lines.</u>

Firstly, I know I've used two phrases to define the same thing, which also has a third label – "lead magnet". Now that you understand what they all mean – as Bookkeeping professionals, let's all agree to call them "welcome lines", ok? Because it evokes helping and solving – rather than selling.

Your welcome lines are your opportunity to provide great value and deliver genuine help to your PC's and start a relationship that will be rewarding for both of you.

When you created your menu, you mapped out the journey from problem to pay off, and your welcome lines are the products that fit into the early stages of that journey.

You can make your welcome lines whatever you like, but my favourites are:

- Accounting file health check
- Diagnostic tools
- eBooks
- Consultations

So let's look at these in a bit more detail.

Accounting file health checks are low-cost offerings that require your PC's details, so they enter your database. You might already be doing these as part of your initial consultation, your needs analysis – and if you are, awesome. You've got yourself a key lead line.

A file health check solves many problems in its own right, because it provides the entrepreneur with much needed clarity.

The key to using the file health check as a welcome line is to convey its value by giving it a price tag. That is, make it a productised service and feature it in your menu, with a price attached. That way, if you strategically give one away, the PC you're helping understands the value you're giving them.

Don't be afraid to show this product to your PC's and encourage uptake of it before diving into your core products.

Diagnostic tools are like scorecards, which I provide at no cost. I give PC's simple quizzes that score the participant over a range of criteria, and then use the scores to offer insights into the health of their financials and/or business.

The process alone offers valuable insights into the health of their business, providing the PC with a new level of clarity around their practices and their financial status.

When you discuss their scores, offer some advice around what you recommend they do in the circumstances. Give them some general advice as part of your value approach, but also suggest they book a complimentary consultation so you can review their results and offer more personalised recommendations.

eBooks are powerful welcome lines. To create one, put together a short, illustrated guide on a subject related to problems you know your PC's struggle with (like cash flow) and give them away free. An eBook not only provides your PC's with incredible value as an educational resource, they can use it to improve their business. And it increases your profile at the same time – as a published author.

When you join The Strategic Bookkeeper Transformation Program, we have a streamlined process whereby you and I co-author my ebook welcome line - The 7 deadly cash flow sins. It's a strategy that works incredibly well and allows you to gain instant profile and credibility as an author.

Consultations may seem obvious to you, as you need to offer PC's a consultation in order for them to get to know you, right? Not really, no. To rinse and repeat – these days your PC's tend to get to know you online. In fact, they get to spend tons of time with you online, more than you could ever offer in a free consultations.

Once a PC gets to know you online – whether that takes 5 minutes or 5 years – a consultation is potentially their next step on your product ladder from content to welcome lines. A consultation may be the first lead line they pick up, or it might not because they might have read your ebook or used your diagnostic tool.

If they do choose a consultation, your purpose is to get more specific about the PC in a one on one situation lasting about 30 minutes. It's a chance to conduct a needs analysis, ask and answer questions and ultimately propose tailored solutions. It's not just a meet and greet, because they feel like they already know you from their online interactions with you!

I prefer to do my consultations face to face via zoom rather than over the phone, but the phone works too.

My Attraction Playbook.

I've saved the best of these assets until last. I've put together a very easy to use and helpful *Attraction Playbook* for you to use – free – to create your attraction strategies.

You can download it for free here: https://www.thestrategicbookkeeper.global/bookresources.[5]

It will take you through every step of building an effective resource of attraction strategies, from how to get started in business networking to putting together a powerful profile.

It also covers some of the concepts we've already covered, like product ladders and welcome lines, to strategies we'll talk about below, including:

- Evergreen Advocacy Partnerships (EAP's)
- Results Based Marketing
- Social Media
- Market Segmentation
- Keep in Touch Marketing
- Key Website Pages
- SEO
- Google Adwords

[5]URL: https://thestrategicbookkeeper.s3.ap-southeast-2.amazonaws.co m/TSB+Attraction+Playbook.pdf

Your attraction building strategies.

Okay, we've talked about a number of attraction concepts and tools and examined the brand and attraction assets you'll need to have in place to make your attraction strategies work, so it's time to discuss some seriously powerful strategies that I've developed.

Evergreen Advocacy Partnerships.

Evergreen Advocacy Partnerships are the business in terms of client attraction, my friends! But before we dive into the *what, why* and *how*, of the EAP (Evergreen Advocacy Partnership), I'd first like to explore "referral relationships".

Referral Relationships

Similar to advocacy marketing, which we discussed earlier, referral relationships are pretty simple right? You meet, you get along, you identify that referring clients to each other is mutually beneficial, and you agree that when the opportunity arises, you'll send business to one another.

Referral relationships can be awesome if you cultivate and nurture them. The more value you give, the more you get.

If you've tried referral relationships and they haven't worked for you, I'd say it's because there's no firm foundation for the relationship. It's a loose arrangement where the roles of the two parties are undefined and the rewards are uncertain.

On the whole, referral relationships are not strategic, and they're passive rather than active.

EAP's, on the other hand...

Evergreen Advocacy Partnerships (EAP's for short), on the other hand, are both strategic and active. The partners in an EAP seek to actively build each other's brands, so that they grow and prosper together. An EAP has a strategy and an agenda. It's more of a formal arrangement than a referral relationship.

And if you're thinking to yourself that you've never heard of Evergreen Advocacy Partnerships before, it's because they're brand new. You won't read or hear about them anywhere else, because they're part of my IP, which I'm happy to share with you.

Why the name "Evergreen Advocacy Partnership"

Well, evergreen means "enduring", advocacy means "recommend" and partnership means "joint ownership". And this special relationship is about all those things.

It's about joint ownership of an enduring relationship which seeks to build advocacy for one another's brands. It's about growing your client base together.

So how does it work?

Well again, you're looking for partners with whom you can grow.

But at the bottom, an EAP is about solving problems for your PC's and VIP's by leveraging the expertise of carefully selected partners – and giving those partners access to your expertise in return.

To begin with, let's rinse and repeat for a moment.

"If I provide you with value in order to help you do better in business then you'll advocate for my brand, and eventually you may also do business with me."

So how does this work in terms of setting up Evergreen Advocacy Partnerships? Well firstly, you're looking for partners with whom you can grow.

Say you're at an event, or just talking to someone – it can be a client, it can be a perfect stranger – and a problem or issue they're grappling with comes up. If it's not something you can help with directly, then you advocate for someone who can.

You say, "I have a referral partner, Business X, and they do a really great job of that, and I'd be happy to get in touch with them on your behalf." And the relationship is born. They're now in your sphere. If the result comes out the way they wanted, they're on their way to becoming your advocates.

So how do you find these partners?

Well, the natural place to start is on your database. Clients make great potential EAP's – but not just because they're clients. You need to evaluate them on their merits first. Will your expertise be useful to them to pass on to their network, and will their expertise be useful to you to pass on? If so, by all means pursue an EAP.

Think about the businesses that the people you meet will need. B2B service businesses who serve the same market as you do – digital marketing agencies like website designers, social media, graphic designers etc. Then there are allied businesses like accountants, debt collectors, pre-insolvency firms, HR practices, money lenders, insurance brokers, banks and this list goes on. It's all about seeing the opportunity and having the opening to form the partnership.

I've found EAP's at face-to-face networking events and online. A great place to look is on Facebook business groups. But the truth is you can find them anywhere. I've met great EAP's in all manner of places and when I least expected it.

You can cold call businesses to obtain EAP's if you want to – I haven't but I won't stop you doing it. If you see someone you really want as an EAP, reach out to them.

What to do once you've found your potential EAP.

The first step is to ask for a meeting.

You can reach out by email or phone (or even text message), it's easy and I've included a script in my *Attraction Playbook:*

Subject Line: Referral Relationship

Email Body: Hi John. Would you have 15 minutes to catch up on zoom to discuss how we might form a mutually beneficial referral relationship?

*I highly recommend adding a link to your calendar to allow them to act immediately and book in with you.

The meeting.

The first meeting is a quick catch up to find out a few key things:

a) Do we serve the same target market?
b) Do you have a product or service that I really want to recommend to my clients?
c) Do we share values – as in, do we click human to human?

Be ready.

Rule number one here is, don't go in cold. Have an agenda ready. Not necessarily a script, but a list of things you want to talk about.

The kind of questions you want to ask are things like, "Who do you serve, and what problems do you solve?" That will tell you whether your potential partner has a similar database, or if they're serving clients that you can't help, which might change the tone.

But if that's the case, don't just cut it off, because there might still be some value. They might say, "Well, your clients can probably use us, but we can't use you." But if you think they're amazing, you might say, "Oh my goodness, all my clients need you."

So that might prompt them to say, "Well for every client that you refer, we'll give you a fee or something." Beautiful things happen if you just listen and seek to understand. So listen, and probe for points of agreement. Don't worry too much about anything else –just start by getting to know them and then tell them about you.

Now, as this all unfolds, you're going to start to get a gut feel for whether this person is someone that you want to move forward with. If you do, consider the issue of exclusivity. With some of my partners I insist on it being exclusive, but it depends on the partner, so for some I don't.

Setting up the next meeting.

Respect each other's time. Keep it within the 15 minutes you asked for, and then decide if you want to take it further. If you don't, you could say, "I've learnt a lot today John, let me digest all that, think about how I could serve you best and get back to you"

If you do, then you could say, "John, I think we'd make great referral partners. Would you be interested in exploring this a bit further?" If the answer is yes, "Ok great, I think we'll need about 30 minutes, which we can do now or another time, which suits you best?"

The second meeting.

If the first meeting is going well and you've both got time, you can progress to this meeting immediately rather than booking another time.

It's at this point that you'll introduce "John" to the EAP (which will probably blow his mind). Explain that referral relationships are great, but *Evergreen Advocacy Partnerships* are next level and yield greater results over the long term.

Then set out the agenda:

1. Agree to meet regularly – how often depends on how deep the relationship

is or becomes, but it can be monthly, bi-monthly, or perhaps quarterly.

2. If my team (or yours) is best placed to do the referring, then we'll make introductions – in some cases that's really important.
3. If I believe my team will be able to serve our clients by understanding my EAP's value (which ultimately is how they'll solve a problem) then I will set up a meeting.

Impress them with your structure.

I've designed several different levels of interaction with your EAP's, which you can discuss with your potential EAP if the meeting continues. The levels are: *Level 1* – both parties simply agree to refer each other when they have the chance. Your teams need to meet each other, which helps your tribes to understand why each other's services are of value. At this point, you should set up a regular (leaders) meeting schedule.

Level 2 – you introduce them to your database via email or other mediums like social media, podcasts and more – using the value approach to endorse them asking that they do the same for you.

Level 3 – next, you could integrate them into your new client onboarding process. If this seems appropriate (remember, use the value approach) then go for it – and perhaps they can do that for you too. If you introduce a new client to an EAP who helps them do better in business or life, this will deepen their advocacy for your brand.

Level 4 – you actually integrate each other's products into your offerings. As an example, let's say you're partnered with a debt consolidation agency who are able to offer your clients a diagnostic tool, free information and a free consultation with personalised recommendations – all obligation free with the value approach at its heart – what a great way to stack the value of your "product" and give you yet another competitive advantage. And vice versa using your welcome lines.

As a Strategic Bookkeeper, you'll have the capacity to do all these things because your database will be set up, segmented and managed (which we'll discuss in detail below in the *Keep in Touch Marketing* section), you'll be sending out onboarding emails (and videos and texts) and you'll have developed "products" full of value.

To rinse and repeat – an EAP is about solving problems for your clients by leveraging the expertise of carefully selected partners – and them doing the same with you.

Partnerships like this are all around us, and the potential power they have has been proven over and over again. Look at Ikea partnering with Lego, Nike and Michael Jordan, Taco Bell and Doritos, Amazon and American Express.

You can harness a similar power by learning and developing your own EAP's on a scale that suits your practice.

If your EAP has an eBook or a health check – or another welcome line – that would genuinely serve your clients, and you serve it up using the value tool, you can't go wrong. If your EAP has a product (it doesn't matter if it's a welcome line or a core product) that you can integrate into your product ladder to add value, gain a competitive advantage or increase your profile, why wouldn't you?

What if you landed an EAP with your local bank manager – what kind of power and profile could come from that?

Be selective.

When you advocate for someone else, that relationship is on you. Say you refer a friend, or worse, a VIP, to an advocate partner, and they have a terrible experience. Your friend or client will now be questioning your judgement and they'll find it hard to trust anything you say ever again.

So it's crucial that you have the utmost faith in your advocacy partners at all levels. Some people will give you more than you give them and vice versa and that's okay. But what's not okay is that you advocate for someone who underperforms. So my advice here is to focus on the value your referrals are giving, and always remember to occasionally stop, take a big breath, and reflect on what's working and what's not working.

Find your top three that really give you the most and nurture them and make them know that they're special to you. On the other hand, if a relationship is not delivering value to you, cut it off. Sometimes it's just as important in business to stop doing some things as it is to continue doing others.

A rinse and repeat respite.

If you're feeling a bit fatigued, take a breath and let's rinse and repeat for a moment. Client attraction is a big subject, and you're not going to master all this all at once. So please don't try.

We're over halfway through this pretty huge chapter, so read on. Finish the book, use my playbooks, and commit to playing the long game. And please tune into my podcast because on there I have the time to dive into client attraction strategies in more depth.

Put one foot in front of the other in the direction of success and you'll get there, I promise.

Results Based Marketing.

As an early adopter in the tech, business and economic landscapes generally, I've always kept my finger on the pulse and been an early adopter. I was one of the first to create a proper website, and early to invest in building genuine 5-star reviews.

So results based marketing – using reviews, testimonials and case studies to build trust, credibility and profile – is one of the key ways I built my practice from the early days up until recently.

Research has shown that consumers trust online reviews as much as they trust a referral from a family or friend, so having a consistently high approval rating and reviews can really help to build your competitive advantage.

How to make it happen.

Generating the reviews and testimonials you need is fairly easy. All you need to do is jump on Google, set your practice up as a Google Business and encourage your VIP's to share their reviews online so you can help people achieve the same results you've achieved for them. We always request a review when we complete a product program for a client. We have a process of constantly gathering reviews.

Showcase the results you get from these reviews on social media posts, and always point PC's to your results on your website. That means having at least a few prominently displayed on the home screen, and a link to more.

A caveat.

For quite a while before the pandemic hit, our VIP's were mainly local businesses only. It seemed that many entrepreneurs were more comfortable with a local bookkeeper even if they never saw us in person. We were getting 1-2 new enquiries per week leveraging our reputation, using results-based marketing – Google reviews

Here's the thing, when covid hit, for whatever reason, the effectiveness of our results-based marketing changed – which is testament to "what works today might not necessarily work as well tomorrow."

There are "principles" in sales and marketing that stand the test of time - principles like the ones I'm teaching you in this book. Building a great reputation is a timeless marketing principle - and just good business, right? But how it works, over time changes.

That's why I've structured the The Strategic Bookkeeper Transformation Program so we can continue to support you with new and updated information and assets – to stay at the top of your game.

Social media.

Earlier we had a *short digression into social media*. Now let's look at it in more detail.

I know a lot of bookkeepers are wondering about the value of social media as a client attraction tool. You're probably wondering, "does it work?" "Should I be doing it?" "How do I make it work?" "Do I need to spend money on it?"

Well, I'm here to answer all these questions – and my *Attraction Playbook* includes a social media section, so you'll find more direct actions there.

Does it work?

Yes it does – that's why so many people do it – but maybe not in the way you imagine it does. For me, social media is an exercise in branding, not direct sales. It works as "content" in your product ladder, so it helps your PC's to get to know, like and trust you. So it's an important part of your long game strategy.

Should I be doing it?

Yes, it's a must – but you don't need to be a slave to it. As I said, it's not a direct sales activity, and the returns will become evident over time. So don't bother spending hours and hours on your social media believing it's the holy grail – it's not.

How do I make it work?

There's a step-by-step instruction in my *Attraction Playbook*, so be sure and work through it when you decide to invest some energy into social media. The platforms that I recommend highly are Facebook, Instagram, LinkedIn, Google Business and YouTube – although if you're not going to create any videos just yet, leave that last one for now.

If you use tech tools like Hootsuite, you can post across all your platforms with one push of a button, so there's no need to go and repeat the same thing everywhere.

Your frequency and content strategy.

Map out how often you'll post, and what you'll post about. Remember, you always need to serve up valuable content that seeks to help your audience with one thing or another – even if it's just to boost their mood.

Remember, bookkeeping is the vehicle – not the destination or the holiday – so consider what you can post that relates to helping your audience do better in business more generally. Tap into your mountain of value and express your brand personality. You'll find that you've got stuff to say – not just about bookkeeping – and social media is a great place to say it.

Who's your audience?

On social media, invite your friends, family and business buddies to follow and like you. Ask them "do you know someone who runs a business who feels a bit stuck", or something like that. Be general in your enquiry – it doesn't always have to be about the bookkeeping.

That said, bookkeeping could be the vehicle that gets them to destination "unstuck" – and you might have a lovely welcome line (aka lead line) consultation that opens the floor for Q & A and seeks to help them get there.

Engagement is a two-way street.

So you've been on socials now for a few months, you're ticking the boxes (on your plan) and getting more followers on each platform. Guess what – you've now got a room full of people (a bit like at a networking event) who "know" you. So get to know them. Read their profiles, and you might find new opportunities you missed before. Be genuine, seek to understand, and find ways you can be of value so that when you engage with your followers it's meaningful.

Should I be spending money on it?

We'll cover that shortly in my section on paid advertising, but for now the short answer is no.

Boosting posts and paying for other forms of social media rarely results in *direct sales* for Bookkeepers. At best, it can be a way to direct some people to your website, and get them to float into your brandsphere. However, there can be value in paid forms of social media and so if and when you're ready to try that as part of your overall attraction strategies, apply the same rules I've outlined for Google AdWords.

Consistency is the key.

One thing I recommend you do is occasionally post on your personal social media profiles – in order to let your network know that you would love to help them do better in business. And, to ask them to support you to do better in business too. If you're shy about this, ask yourself why? I'm not asking you to throw your business cards unsolicited at your friends, I'm suggesting you seek to be of service and to be supported – which are both beautiful things.

You could post "Hey friends, I'm building up my business socials and I'd be all smiles if you'd like and follow my page here" and.... "Hey friends, I don't often post business stuff on my personal page but in this case, I wanted to share my ebook with my business buddies in case it helps even one of you – so here is a small gift from me to you – the 7 deadly cashflow sins – it's a fast read and a "how to" book. Enjoy".

And I recommend using Canva to create your posts.

Remember that all of this contributes to bringing more people into your brandsphere so that they can digest your content, opt into your welcome lines, get value, become advocates and tell others.

A social media story.

This story illustrates the power of social media and at the same time shows how all my attraction strategies work together in harmony, and all the ingredients in my secret sauce method work together too.

Let me tell you about Peter. He is a classic case of someone who floated into my brandsphere. I was able to nurture him in an online way, and today we're great business buddies and he's a source of excellent business for me.

Peter and I met in a business setting and decided to connect personally on social media, and because of this he started following my business socials. Before he did that, he didn't know that much about me – he knew I was a bookkeeper but that's about all. But online, he was able to get to know me (professionally) in his own time, by absorbing my content – content which was advocating for my brand.

He read my eBook and eventually decided to book a free consultation to "continue the conversation".

Peter told me he was thinking about buying a franchise and that he wanted to use the consultation to "chew the fat" on the idea. Not to seek formal advice on acquisition – but just as a sounding board.

So we jumped into an online meeting, and I just listened to him. And after a while, I began to ask questions. Nothing too probing, just natural, obvious questions. And through that Q & A (even though he was the one coming up with the answers), it was as though a light had been switched on for him. He got much needed clarity and we both had tons of fun, deepening our relationship along the way.

All in the space of just over 30 minutes.

At the end he expressed his gratitude by saying "I can't believe that was a free session, I got so much value out of it, thank you."

Sometime shortly after, he bought the franchise, and then he reached out again to ask me what I recommended in terms of bookkeeping. I showed him our menu and suggested a welcome package (file set up and initial bookkeeping) which he jumped at. After one of my team of bookkeepers completed the initial job, I caught up with him again to recommend core and succession products.

Peter's a smart guy. He's organised and capable, and he knows his way around Xero. So we determined he'd do the day to day bookkeeping himself and we'd support him with a DIY Bookkeeper Support package (a core product) plus monthly virtual CFO (a succession product).

Soon after that I sent him a personal text message to say Happy Birthday, which led to him sharing some great news, he'd broken even after only 8 weeks in business – phenomenal for a startup!

I jumped on the phone and called him. Say what! That's incredible! I shared his excitement and celebrated his success, and I asked him "Hey Peter, I don't suppose you'd consider jumping on zoom and going into a bit more detail would you? It's just that I'm pretty sure that your success story could be of massive value to other business owners, and I'd love to capture it."

He said yes and we did it, and it was amazing. And he gave me permission to share it freely on social media and via email. I thought, "I don't care if anyone likes this. It's not about me, it's about the value it can bring to others. If this helps one person, I'm keen."

Peter called me a week later and he said, "Guess what happened?" He'd shared the video with the franchise HQ, who loved it so much they featured it all over the place, and they tagged my business. Not only did I get some great free press, but my followers increased, and another plumber reached out shortly after and became a client too.

Peter also informed me that a plumber had spotted the video, reached out to him and said "I'm sick of working for myself. I want to come work for you and bring all of my clients." To say he was thrilled is an understatement.

And it all happened because I sought to help someone do better in business using the advocacy approach.

Peter is still a client and a wonderful business buddy. During the interview I discovered his passion for what he calls a "people first approach" which is another name for "advocacy marketing" – which he cited as one of the key ways he broke even in just 8 weeks.

I love to share that story.

But wait, as they say in the ads, there's more. Sometime shortly after, another business buddy (also a plumber) booked a consultation to discuss how he too could do better in business. He was self-employed and struggling, and he was toying with the idea of giving it all up and getting a job – but he really didn't want to.

I suggested that perhaps, based on Peter's experience, he should explore the same franchise model – and I referred him to the franchise HQ. And of course, they know me because I've created amazing collateral for them, as well as now sending them a potential franchisee. All because I wanted to give value, not with any ulterior motive. And now they want to partner with me nationally to refer all their franchises to me.

So can you see how this advocacy approach is the gift that keeps on giving. How all the principles described in Advocacy Marketing come together and work together. How all the ingredients in my secret sauce recipe work together.

It all works together.

I can't think of a better way to illustrate how my strategies all work together in a kind of wonderful synergy. And that's why The Strategic Bookkeeper Transformation

Program isn't just a course or any other static system – it's a complete program and a tribe that seeks to continue the journey together. And when it changes, which it always does, we can all change and adapt together.

KIT marketing – Keep in Touch.

Social media is a great way of expanding your database and once you begin to bring people in – that is VIP's, PC's, accountants, EAP's and so on, it's important to keep in touch with them. And the way to do that is through KIT (Keep in Touch) marketing.

KIT marketing is actually a *critical driver* of your client attraction *targets*. It's an activity that you do regularly in order to drive a specific result – we'll talk more about *critical drivers* later.

An example of KIT marketing and its benefits: I use automation software to reach out to my network of accountants once every three months just to say hi, to remind them that they can book in time with me to discuss how we might refer more work to each other – and bookings pop up in my calendar like magic. Well, like the result of good strategy, right?

This is just one example with one segment of your database. Another great example of KIT marketing is birthday messages. I send automated birthday emails and I also send a personal text message too – this is an exercise in "never forget your customers and they'll never forget you", it's good manners and it will improve retention rates (when combined with all the other ingredients).

You'd be surprised the kind of responses you'll get from thoughtful birthday text messages – the joy it can bring to a clients day.

With KIT marketing, the possibilities are endless, and my playbook is designed to help you step by step.

Segmenting your database.

We sell three different packages across two different product ranges, so we use six tags for our clients. In *Succession* we'll talk about how this allows us to tailor our communication to our VIP's in a way that informs them on how we can help them solve even more problems.

We've also created separate segments for groups such as prospects, past clients, accountants, advocacy partners and so on. And we can send every one of those groups automated messages.

That said, it's important to keep in touch with your prospects, clients and partners by sending them bespoke, valuable, genuine emails, text message and phoning them. So you can't automate everything.

You need a combination of both.

Why is that Jeannie?

Many reasons, one being that email is not 100% reliable, they can land in junk or spam or simply be left unread. But also because you want to ask specific questions of specific people – so a personal text message for example is often ideal. For example, let's say a PC read your ebook and had a consultation with you a few months ago, it's good manners to send a personal text and ask a question about their situation like "Hi Sam, I thought of you today. How's everything going? Did you manage to get caught up on the books? Jeannie". That message shows you care and seeks to serve Sam – you're keeping in touch with him so that he can keep in touch with you and take action when the time is right. This has generated business for me and it will for you too.

Won't they think I'm pestering them?

Actually, quite the opposite. It's actually helpful. This is not about spamming your database with advertising, it's about nurturing relationships, giving value, seeking to serve, being well mannered and giving them the power (and the actual way) to reach out to you when they are ready.

Some time ago I had my car detailed. He did such a great job, I was thrilled. A few months later I needed my car cleaned again but I couldn't find his number. If only he had a keep in touch marketing system where I received a monthly text message and a link to book in – how convenient and valuable would that be.

Sports betting fans want their KIT hourly!

The key to KIT marketing (and all my marketing principles) is not to think of them as marketing at all – think value, think building relationships, think solving problems – it's not about selling, it's about being of service. Once again, you're a solver not a seller.

All my marketing strategies are aimed at being win-win's. That's the value approach.

Don't get overwhelmed but do get excited by the extent of KIT's power.

Simply begin the journey of keeping in touch with people. Do your laps around the sun, lean in and work smart. When you need to, reach out for support in our free Facebook group *The Strategic Bookkeepers Way*, where you can network with other people who are on the same journey as you.

The bigger your database, the more opportunities exist for you to do "daily things" to drive client attraction. Could you reach out to one accountant a day or a week? Could you send a thoughtful message enquiring about a past client once a day or week? Could you connect one new EAP a day or a week? What are five activities you could do around KIT that would move the needle? Put them in a spreadsheets – make them your norms, your critical drivers – and drive the results you want.

Key website pages.

Let's shift gears a bit and return to your website. Back in the *Attraction assets* section I emphasised how critical your website is to your practice, which I'm sure you already knew.

But by now, after reading this far, I'm guessing you have a few ideas about how your website should look. You need to have positive reviews up front and visible, your profile has to be accessible, your awards and qualifications should be prominently displayed, and so on.

In my *Attraction Playbook* you'll find a list of key website pages that I highly recommend you include on your site, because each of them has value for your brand.

Are you optimised?

While we're talking about your website, we should probably cover the topic of optimisation. Or to use its full name, Search Engine Optimisation (SEO).

If you Google the definition of SEO you'll find lots of result, but my definition, which I've formulated especially for Strategic Bookkeepers, is that it's how you optimise your digital assets (often that's your website) which contributes to you being found online, and in searches on search engines like Google.

It can get very technical and it can be easy to get bad advice and be roped into paid SEO without an appropriate understanding of what you're actually paying for, so you need to be careful. Here's how I recommend that you get – and stay – optimised.

Step 1 – Do all the things.

By that I mean do all the things I suggest in this chapter and in this book as a whole. As mentioned above, I adopted early, and I've been ranking high and well for ages. And I did it all by myself, just by being present online with good, high value content.

I've proved that your website and in fact your whole brand will be far better optimised when you invest in providing your market with value through the content you serve up. That includes your website itself, but all your digital assets, from your menu and your online profile, to blogs, Google Reviews, and everything else.

It's critical that you keep your content relevant and up to date. Value and advocacy are two words to imprint on your brain here. If you concentrate on providing value and building advocacy, magic will happen.

Step 2 – use my SEO Guide.

My SEO Guide, which you can download here: https://www.thestrategicbookkeeper.global/bookresources[6] is a really comprehensive guide to ensuring that your content is search engine friendly and effective. I take you through every aspect of creating search engine optimised content, including:

1. Keyword research
2. Readability
3. Creating content
4. Backlinks
5. Google Analytics
6. Page experience

It's a great learning tool, because it combines easy to implement advice around how to write and present your information, with technical detail (and links) around things like the Google Keyword Planner, and ensuring that your site visitors have an easy and enjoyable experience.

Step 3 – If you're considering paying for SEO.

[6]URL: https://thestrategicbookkeeper.s3.ap-southeast-2.amazonaws.co m/SEO+Plan+-+Jeannie+Savag e.pdf

There are lots of SEO service providers who are willing to charge you high and ongoing fees for work that is primarily done at the beginning, so if you're going to pay someone, run them through my checklist. Show them my guide and ask them what their comments are, and if they're going to do all the things I talk about. Also ask them if they will provide:

- A checklist of exactly what they are going to do at the beginning.
- How you can compare your SEO now to your SEO after their phase 1.
- A program of exactly what they're going to do on a weekly basis.
- Proof of any ranking results improvements.

It will cost money.

Decide on your budget and projected ROI before you start. This is a big one that bookkeepers get wrong, because they don't realise that it all comes down to the cost of acquisition. If you're going to spend $X then exactly how many clients per month/year and how much revenue is reasonable to expect as minimum.

My program costs are transparent.

If you join The Strategic Bookkeeper Transformation Program, I expect you to be able to multiply your investment by a factor of ten.

But what about your BAM (bare ass minimum) ROI? Do not spend money on marketing unless you understand this! In terms of my program, you would need to find at least one new client to make your money back. If you also upgrade one existing client you'll probably be in front. That's a BAM ROI. We also offer a money back guarantee on your BAM ROI.

How I can help

SEO is constantly changing. At the time of writing this book my team is vetting SEO experts. We're learning more and what's new – so we can bring this to the members of my program. If you join the program, we'll inform you and help you implement what you learn. If you do decide to pay for SEO – we'll be there to help, to point you to vetted providers with great services that fit your budget – a budget I understand because I'm a Bookkeeper just like you.

Paid advertising.

When I say paid advertising, I'm referring to Google AdWords, also known as Pay Per Click (PPC), which may or may not be combined with paid social media.

The first thing you should know is that this game is pricey. Often, you're competing with people with big budgets, so if you don't have your brand and messaging and pretty much everything else perfect, it's probably not going to work for you.

In my experience, Google AdWords can work, and social media advertising may work in combination with this, but there are a lot of caveats around that. One of those is that I see no evidence that paid social media results in direct, volume sales, although it can drive traffic to your website.

What's it going to cost me?

That's a great question. And one that is rarely answered well in my experience.

One of the main issues here is, how much will it cost to gain a client using PPC advertising, and what is the expected lifetime return of that client?

One of the big mistakes bookkeepers make is spending tons of money, but ultimately not understanding the numbers around PPC / Google Adwords spends required, and falling short.

At the time of writing this book, my research indicates that you will need between $10,000 and $15,000 capital investment to get you through the first three months – including set up and testing, and tweaking. Beyond that first three months, you'll need between $2500 and $3500 per month for the actual advertising plus the management of your campaign, so your annual budget should be a minimum of $30,000 per annum, up to a ceiling of around $42,000.

Even with that level of spend there are no guarantees that you'll find any new clients, but for that money you'd hope you'd find at least one.

Should I do it?

I have never met a bookkeeper or accountant who has built a thriving practice with delighted clients – and is living the dream – through google AdWords.

Because PPC is solely about client attraction, whereas the whole package – the thriving practice, delighted clients, your dream on your terms – is about far more than client attraction. I mean what do you do with the client once you bring them in? How do you nurture a seed into a fully grown fruit tree?

Google AdWords can be a piece of your client attraction puzzle if you decide it's something you want to try (and capital you're willing to risk), but to rinse and repeat, only try it once you have all the elements of my Strategic Bookkeeping secret sauce in place.

My story.

Have I made google AdWords work for my practice? Yes I have.

Would I recommend you do it? Only once you've nailed every aspect of The Strategic Bookkeeper methodology – or it won't work.

After a failed first attempt some time ago in 2015, I went back to Google Adwords and I made it work. Back then, the spend required was about $1500 per month, and it was a lot easier. These days it's a lot harder, for many reasons including the market is more crowded and competitive and the capital investment required is a lot higher.

There's one thing I know, and that is if you learn and employ all my strategies, there's a very good chance that you won't need Google AdWords.

It depends on what your dream is.

Every Bookkeeper has a "point of satisfaction" in terms of her career, her income and her lifestyle. You can pull $250,000 profit out of a small practice with 2-3 staff if you're smart about it.

If you're dreaming of a practice with 10 plus staff and seven figure net profits, then at some point, Google AdWords could work for you if you're willing to sacrifice a bit more time and energy as well as invest more money.

If that's your dream on your terms, go for it. I'll be there every step of the way cheering you on.

The key? Respond. Fast.

If somebody calls you from a Google AdWords campaign and you don't answer, they're not going to leave a message. They're going to move on.

Get your brand spot-on, get your menu perfect, work on all of your attraction strategies so your brand assets are on-point. But then, critically, make sure you're able to respond within seconds to every enquiry.

Phone calls must be answered immediately and can't go to voicemail. Make sure "contact forms" hit your hot little hands the second they land (and don't get lost in the rest of your email).

Trust someone who's done it all. This stuff is easier said than done.

With my other attraction strategies, the people that come through will be ready to do business pretty much immediately, because they've had time to get to know, like and trust you through your advocacy marketing approach. But when they come through Google advertising or social media, they are a lot harder to convert. Plus, obviously you're going to get tyre kickers as well.

Should I go to a marketing agency?

Fast forward to a time when you've nailed all parts of the Strategic Bookkeeping method and your ducks are in a row. You're dreaming of expansion beyond a boutique practice with more than five full time bookkeepers on your team, and you're ready for the work involved.

Then yes, when it comes to paid advertising, Google AdWords, yes. Go ahead and recruit a specialist. That's what I did in 2015 and it's what I recommend to bookkeepers who decide that their dream is a bigger than a boutique practice.

If you're building a boutique practice, which I define as five people or less, I don't think you'll have any use for AdWords – my strategies will fill up your books. Then again, if you hire a specialist agency, there's no guarantee that you'll get results, because Google AdWords is just a part of the puzzle, and all the other pieces need to be in place.

You can absolutely use my strategies to grow your practice to any size without the use of Google AdWords too.

Attraction needs attention.

Attraction is an ongoing process. It's not a tap you can switch on and off, it's a way of life. So it's not something you can "set and forget" either (except for some automated messaging). It's about continual experimentation, refinement, and learning what works and what doesn't.

You have to test how everything works. What return on investment did you get for the time and money that you put into it? How can you change it to make it better? What part needs a tweak?

Testing tells you what to change or improve, and what you need to stop because it's not working.

What you get when you become part of my tribe.

Just to bring this chapter to a close I wanted to give you an insight into the attraction resources and assets that we provide for you when you become part of The Strategic Bookkeeper Transformation Program. Just looking at this list is exhausting, but we really do give you all of these things, ready to use. Plus, we're passionate about updates and new releases because as I'm sure you've noticed, I'm big on future proofing and staying ahead of the game.

- All lead lines (eBook, health checks etc).
- A library of 500 and growing social media post templates.
- A social media strategy and support with how to implement it.
- "Done for you" database and KIT messaging.
- Attraction critical drivers / daily activities / progress trackers.
- How to actually enjoy business networking and make it work.
- Help with your profile.
- Step by step support to create your EAP's and make them work.
- Strategies and scripts to increase your online reviews and results-based marketing.
- Ongoing SEO education, implementation and support
- "Done for you" website pages and some templates you can integrate into your current website – plug and play to hit the ground running.
- Support to understand if and when you're ready to do Google AdWords, and referrals to vetted suppliers.
- Continual updates and new releases – to everything.

Done for your Client Attraction

In 2023 when The Strategic Bookkeeper Transformation Program becomes available to join you'll also gain the benefit of the work our team is doing around done-for-you Client Attraction. Here's how

- A platform with an Academy and a podcast - the podcast featuring global superstar, educating entrepreneurs on why they should work with a Strategic Bookkeeper
- This includes a directory where you'll be listed as a Certified Strategic Bookkeeper
- We are also in discussions with global organisations who have your target audience and we are setting up Evergreen Advocacy Partnerships with them to drive traffic to the podcast and to you

It would be easier to ask what you *don't* get when you become a tribe member. And what it would cost you personally to create, test, refine, perfect and implement on your own.

Phew.

That's a big chapter, so well done for completing it. Let's go on to the next phase, Conversion. I promise, it isn't quite so huge, but it's just as useful.

Chapter 5. The Process of Conversion.

I'm going to make this short and simple: conversion is about helping people. And the first thing you need to do in the conversion process is help your PC's see that what you're providing is value, not a cost.

As bookkeepers in practice, we all know that a lot of clients are cost conscious - and that means they want to compare your hourly rate with that of the practice down the road.

Your brand, your menu and your attraction strategies are all about making PC's look beyond the hourly rate to the way you solve their problems - and the payoff they'll get - to demonstrate your value.

A smart strategic conversion process is about nailing that change in their thinking. Like a friend who sings your praises better than you do, a well thought out conversion system is a way to help your PC's actually see and feel the value you're capable of delivering.

So it's a key ingredient in the recipe for competing on outcomes and value – not price.

You're at a fork in the road.

The conversion point is a real fork in the road, for a couple of reasons.

Firstly because your PC is either going to convert or not convert to a VIP, and whether they do is up to you.

But it may also be a fork in the road for you as a bookkeeper because of your limiting beliefs. You can do the job and you have the power to do incredible things, but you may think you're unable convey that power to your PC's. You say things like, "I'm not comfortable with this, I'm not good at this, I'm no good with the sales and marketing stuff".

In this chapter I'll share a lot of practical conversion strategies, but we'll also work on ways of enhancing your self-belief. Because it's crucial to making conversion work for you.

To rinse and repeat – let's turn your ceiling into your new floor!

If you put a giraffe in an elephant suit does that make the giraffe an elephant? No, it doesn't. She's still a giraffe. You don't need to put on an elephant suit and run around pretending to be something you're not to have success here.

Again – conversion is about helping people, and you're good at that. You are built for this, and you'll succeed because I've built this system for you.

The value approach (again).

Use the value approach end to end in your conversion process – because it's designed to centre you, calm any nerves, and ensure you don't feel like an elephant in a giraffe suit (to continue the metaphor).

When you strip it all back to the value approach, you'll see that you don't need to be a "salesperson". You can be a problem solver seeking to be of value. You can be you.

Focus on what's best for the client.

Sometimes during the needs analysis, I hear myself sounding bossy. I feel like I'm coming off like the Spanish Inquisition. So I pause and say, "I'm sorry if I sound bossy and that I'm asking a lot of questions, there's a method to my madness that helps me get the best outcomes for you."

During the proposal, if I'm giving a PC a choice of three packages, I tell them which one I recommend for them. I say, "I absolutely recommend the *best* package for you because I know that every business owner needs to be held accountable to their numbers. I see the results of doing this and of not doing this every day. That said, the choice is yours. If you chose the *good* package or the *better* package, either will suffice. But it would be remiss of me not to tell you what I recommend for you."

If the value approach is at the heart of what you're doing and you're true to yourself, you can't go wrong.

Taking clients on a journey.

By the time your PC makes contact with you, they are ready to buy. They've been consuming and enjoying your content, maybe they've engaged in a welcome line (which also means you've been keeping in touch with them via automated emails) so you've built up their *know, like* and *trust* stocks in the virtual world.

Now they're ready to take the next step and meet you in the real world – whether that's by phone or zoom or in person.

To rinse and repeat: please consider zoom meetings over "in person". Even if you're time rich now, once you employ The Strategic Bookkeeper principles, you won't be – you'll be full up with clients and time will be your most precious resource. So start as you mean to go on.

What you do next is critical.

Now, I'm sure you know this – very few clients ever come in with clean and tidy books. So they need you to get them out of a mess first.

Whether they've been trying to DIY their bookkeeping or someone else has let them down, they're behind, they're probably stressed, and they're ready to seek help.

You have two conversions ahead of you.

There's the conversion to get them out of the mess they're in. And then, there's the conversion process to turn them into a lifelong VIP.

Tell them why.

Explain your vision for them because it's one in which they'll be better off.

Rinse and repeat time: customers buy 'why' more than 'what'.

Tell them why bookkeeping is important, for example "up to date bookkeeping is globally recognised as pillar one for success because you need to be able to see how your business is performing in terms of profit and cash at all times - so you know what's working and what's not. You can't improve what you're not measuring. That's the value of "bookkeeping" in its own right.

Then turn the conversation to ***Strategic Bookkeeping*** and tell them why it's an investment rather than a cost. How it takes your bookkeeping numbers and uses them in order to actually make and save you money, to optimise your profit and cash. Tell them that really smart business owners know and use their numbers, they sit down every month with an accountability coach, review their results and create an action plan to move the needle.

Your Terms, Your Rules, Your Way.

When you go into the conversion process, it's up to you to determine the terms – the "rules of the game". They're your rules, and they tell the PC how you're going to play to win, so you need to set them down early.

You can find formal terms of trade in the resource section of just about any Bookkeeping Association. If you subscribe to Ignition software like we do, they'll provide you with terms of trade too.

But the kind of terms I'm talking about here are different.

Your terms are first and foremost to ensure your business flourishes. This is about putting yourself first, a concept foreign to many bookkeepers.

When you build your brand and decide who you want to work with, your terms begin to take shape almost organically. Your brand creates your terms and informs your team how to win for the client.

Can you see the synergy?

Your terms are about how you choose to do business and run your practice – and no one but you should determine that. Certainly not your clients.

Your terms include things like the tech both you and your client will use, whether you work onsite or not, the way you'll collaborate with each other, whether you expect payment in advance of the work being done, and so on.

To rinse and repeat, it's about putting yourself first.

You're the heart of your practice, and you need to be happy and healthy – and that's about being comfortable with the way things are built and run. A healthy bookkeeper is a happy (and successful) bookkeeper.

I run my practice like a well-oiled machine. I need my clients to do things my way. I need them to trust me. And when it happens that way, we all go home happy. And honestly, it's my way or the highway.

Once a VIP walks through that velvet rope, they become a VIP and get to enjoy all the benefits and rewards. They agree to trust me, and I take that very seriously. I work my ass off to keep the promises I've made, every day. And I can only do that when we're all playing by my rules.

Be prepared to politely walk away from any PC who doesn't want to play by your rules.

The qualities of a successful converter.

In all my years as a bookkeeper in practice, one thing I've noticed (among many) is the impact five critical qualities have on the bookkeeper/client relationship. These critical qualities will help you in the conversion process and help your team day to day:

- Empathy – Seek to understand before seeking to be understood. Develop empathy for your client first and foremost. Care about them, communicate your understanding, and help them trust that you're committed to helping.
- Belief – The unwavering belief in "your way" and the commitment to have faith in it and be a disciple of it. Your way of working is smart, effective and rewarding – but only if no one tampers with it.

- Confidence – Knowing that you're a skilled, qualified, experienced professional. Be rock solid in your confidence – build it, maintain it and use it to enrol the PC in your process – to become part of your tribe.
- Courage – The resolution to be honest even when it's hard and uncomfortable. To stand by your terms. To say no. And when it's appropriate, to say "hell yes". The courage to trust your gut. The willingness to assert your truths and stand by them, and to walk away if the client doesn't buy into it 100 percent.
- Trust – This is what I call "The Marketing X Factor." There is nothing more important than keeping our promises to our clients. Being reliable and punctual. Doing what we said we would do in the time frame we said we'd do it. Delivering on our commitments.

Stand proud, be confident.

You're a skilled professional. You're entitled to say to your prospective client, "I appreciate you want to do things differently, but I know from experience what happens if I break my own rules. I won't get the outcomes that you need and want, and then you won't be a raving fan. And I only work with raving fans.'"

This is what I call a pineapple conversation.

Pineapple conversations.

Pineapple conversations are prickly, but they aim to get to the juicy centre – which in this case is "only bringing on raving fans".

I get it, they're nerve-wracking. But they're another fork in the road. If you don't have them, you're headed for Painsville. Take the short-term pain for the long term gain.

Because if you accept a client that's trying to take control, is telling you how to do your job, and is not fitting in with your terms, you will absolutely have long term pain.

It will eventually end badly, and it could damage your reputation. They might leave you a bad review. They'll probably take up all your time and suck up your profit too.

Grit your teeth and stand firm. Take control of the relationship and win your clients over to your way of thinking with results, and it will work out better for everyone.

My way v the old way.

Some time ago one of our VIP's had come to the end of their catch up job and required a proposal for ongoing support, as is standard in our practice. My EA, well-meaning at the time, instructed the bookkeeper in charge of the job to prepare and present a proposal to the client, which she did.

The problem is that the bookkeeper was not trained in how to present a proposal using our menu. And so she presented her recommendations – the *what* – the Bookkeeping Package and its investment.

So what's wrong with that? Well, if you've been listening, you'll know that we don't start with what, we start with *why*!

The client thanked her and informed her he'd be DIY'ing his bookkeeping from now on.

I got in touch with the client, and they were kind enough to agree to a second chance. Using the process below, I started with *why*, using our menu. That VIP chose the highest value package out of 3 packages on offer, plus they were full of gratitude for the holistic approach I took – it helped them get much needed clarity in order to make the best decision.

So why the stark difference? One word – communication. By starting with *why* and using our menu, I was able to communicate our value and how it would help them do better in business. Without changing anything about the services on offer, I simply circled back around from the "what" and started again with *why* – and that's how I converted them.

My thought leadership works, my friends. And that's why I strongly recommend you do it my way.

Your conversion strategies.

Now let's get into the actual conversion process. I am going to give you a four-step system that guides you through the method I have developed and used successfully for years.

To rinse and repeat – read this through once, and when you've completed the whole book, go back to the beginning and start working through the techniques I give you in every chapter.

Step 1 – The needs analysis.

The attraction process is complete, and the PC is ready to become a VIP. When they come to you, these PC's really want to be convinced. They've spent enough time with you online to know/like/trust you, and they want their judgement to be proven correct.

This is your opportunity to demonstrate that you speak "client" fluently. To put the five qualities noted above to use, and to create the belief that you are the person who can solve the PC's problems.

The good news is that a needs analysis – the technical Q & A around what they need – is exactly what you're built for. In around 30 minutes or less you can diagnose their problems and start telling them the *why* of what you'll do for them.

Question one.

One of my favourite ways to start is by asking "tell me about your business". It's a broad question that will usually help you find out a whole lot of things that will be relevant to your initial proposal, as well as issues that will feed into subsequent proposals and succession products. You might need to add further prompts like, "what's your vision?" and "what are your personal goals?"

Beyond those open-ended questions, I recommend you use a checklist to ensure you gather all the information you will need to create a proposal. Because checklists are awesome!

Listen carefully.

The answers you get will help you form a picture of this PC as a VIP. Now is the time to stay true to your rules, listen to your gut, and determine if you think this person is the right fit. Because if you're not declining the time-wasters, tyre-kickers and pains in the backside that only want help on their terms, then you're really going to be bringing on pain. Remember, the 80/20 rule: 20% of clients will take up 80% of your time if you let them. You know you can identify them before that happens, so don't be afraid to reject a client.

By the end of the meeting, you should have made a decision about whether to proceed and gathered all the information you'll need to propose a solution and calculate the investment required. But it's very important not to make any recommendations or talk about prices at this stage.

Salespeople spit out prices. Solvers carefully consider needs and make recommendations.

You need to take the time to digest all the information and the personal impressions you've received before you go any further. One of the rules of the game I need you to adopt is, never offer solutions at the first meeting. Trust in the process my friends and magic will happen.

Step 2 – Prepare your recommendations.

This is the technical part, which I'm sure you're already very good at – preparing a formal proposal.

This contains all the detail of the tasks, features and functions of the Service Level Agreement (SLA) you're recommending, and the client engagement letter that will formalise the relationship.

It's not the place to present a list of services and prices. It's all about recommending which of your *products* you recommend – because they're the ones that are going to solve the problems the PC has told you about in the needs analysis.

If I'm proposing ongoing bookkeeping, I'll propose three packages as follows:

- One package which includes traditional Bookkeeping.
- One that includes a quarterly virtual CFO session.
- One that includes monthly virtual CFO.

We use Ignition software, which is designed for accounting businesses, to put our proposals together. Ignition includes a feature that allows us to offer up three packages to our clients.

And in most cases, with my hand on my heart, I recommend the package with the monthly virtual CFO. In the next chapter, on succession, we'll dive even deeper into this, and I'll show you why proposing three options rather than just one works best, and how to set that up.

Step 3 – Deliver your proposal.

This is where the conversion process really gets going.

First, take a deep breath, switch on your courage and confidence, and rely on the value approach.

Say to yourself, *"this is not about me, it's about the value I am determined to deliver to this client, today."*

Before we start.

This process calls for using your website. If you don't have a website or for any reason you don't want to use your website, you can work around it. Maybe make an online brochure that contains all the elements we talk about below.

In this process I'm going to show you parts of one of my scripts. I don't use exactly the same script every time, but I do use the same checklist every time. Modify the script to suit your practice – I'm sure it will be a bit different to mine.

This is your first lap around the sun using my conversion process, so give it time. Refine it on the stone of the market – lean in, learn and let me know how you go.

Use the Loom screen record video app.

I recommend you use the Loom video screen record tool for this part of the process. You can do the whole process "live" on zoom with the client present, but there's no room for error there.

note: putting your face in the video is completely optional, not essential.

Loom will allow you to record the whole proposal delivery using a checklist and a script and start again if you f*#k up. And it's ok to f*#k up. Practice makes perfect.

I like to start my video recording on my website home page, with all the other pages open in other tabs, ready to flick over to them at each part of the process. If you don't have a website, use the online brochure you've created. When you do that, you don't have to be up front all the time – just use your voice.

Start with their first name.

Greet your PC using their first name. "Hi Tom, ok, I've prepared your proposal and now I'm going to walk you through it. Firstly, a bit about us and how we work."

It's critically important to use the PC's first name throughout, and we'll rinse and repeat on that later.

Tell them where they can keep accessing your content.

Remind them that they can find out more in their own time – "Most of the things you need to know about us can be found on our website, which is current and up to date. If you subscribe to my mailing list, I'll occasionally keep you up to date without clogging your inbox."

Talk about your reputation.

It can be helpful to remind the PC of your reputation. "As you may know, we have a five-star reputation on Google, as you can see here. We're very proud of this. Many of these reviews are recent, and actually come from clients who faced the same problems as you."

Don't get caught up in how many reviews you have – work with what you've got – be proud of what you've achieved so far. And of course, when you mention your Google rating (or any other of the pages you mention), show the relevant page.

Refer them to your profile.

We discussed developing your profile using the resources I've included in the *Attraction Playbook* in a past chapter – now is the time to bring it to the forefront as a competitive advantage. "We are award winning bookkeepers recognised by Women in Finance and Xero."

Show them your menu.

Now you'll need your menu. Remember I talked about "showing them your value?" Your menu is a massive part of that. And one of the great things about this digital asset is that it works as a script that steers you away from feature/function language and towards problem/solution language.

To be honest, even I revert back to features and functions without it.

"Here's how we work. First, my team and I are crystal clear on our vision for you, which is X. To achieve that vision, we're on a mission to X. When business owners reach out to us it's usually because they can relate to one or more of these problems XXXXX."

Note that the objective here is to insert the payoffs, and here's how we do just that: "We start here at stage 1, where we..."

Tip: keep all this brief and big picture – avoid talking about tasks or features or functions.

"After that we progress you to stage 2, where we..." and so on.

Show them the whole menu but don't try and sell them the whole kit and kaboodle straight away.

If you're proposing a File Health check and that fits into stage 1, then touch on the other stages so they know what the entire journey looks like. But be sure and let them know that we need to get through stage 1 before we spend too much time thinking about anything else.

You're building comfort and trust, step by step.

When you guide them through your menu step by step, and lead them to the payoffs, you're assuring them that you know what you're doing and building their trust in your experience.

If you're proposing an ongoing bookkeeping engagement and that fits into stage 2 or 3, then don't try and sell the succession stage right away. Show them the whole journey so they know what the possibilities are, but tailor the process to the proposal at hand (the ongoing bookkeeping).

Showing them the whole journey will help you upgrade them to the next thing they need *when they need it* as a succession product.

See how well your menu works?

This is where you discover the true power of your menu which, to rinse and repeat, consists of your Vision, your Mission and your OPS (one page solution). You should want to run through the hills singing about it – show it off like it's a newborn child, because actually, it is the first born child of your brand.

Do you have a guarantee?

Having a guarantee is a great way to increase your perceived value. Your value is only as tangible as how your market perceives it, and a guarantee is proof that you stand behind your work and your value.

If you don't currently have a guarantee, you can leave this part out for now, and challenge yourself to come up with one later. Ask yourself what you're actually doing and not telling your clients, that you could frame up as a guarantee.

The technical proposal.

Now it's time to show them the functions and features and the investment – the SLA.

We use Ignition software, so at this point my video begins to capture the "client view" just as they'll see it, as I walk them through it.

For most bookkeepers, the technical proposal is their entire conversion process – but as you can see here, in The Strategic Bookkeeper method, it's just one small part.

If your whole conversion process revolves around the features and functions of your SLA and the client engagement letter (aka your proposal) then you are definitely going to miss opportunities. And that means you are not going to convert as many PC's to VIP's – you're not going to be able help as many people.

Talk about your capacity.

Creating the perception that there is some urgency around making a decision is an old school, timeless marketing principle. Commenting on your capacity can allude to scarcity, which can help PC's to understand that they need to make a decision quickly – and that's a conversion tool all on its own.

You could say something like this: "Great bookkeepers are in high demand, and so while we currently have the capacity to take on this job for you, we would encourage you to make a decision sooner rather than later as we do have a first-in-best-dressed policy."

If you are literally almost full up, tell them – as long as you use the value tool you can't go wrong. But don't go too far. I'd argue that failing to tell them you only have room for 1 or 2 or 3 more clients is poor customer service. They won't be very happy if they miss out because you omitted that information.

Finish with their name

Finish by ensuring you use their name again. By now, I hope you can see why you should be using their name the whole way through. Yes, because there's a sales-psychology behind that, but also because it's just good manners.

"Well Tom, that's everything. Thank you for your time, I know it's valuable. I'll reach out in a few days to follow up, bye for now."

Step 4 – follow up.

Immediately after you send the proposal video (which we embed in our Ignition software proposal and send all at once), send a text message which reads something like this: *"Hi Tom, I just sent your proposal to you as promised. If you don't see it please check junk or spam. And if you have questions, sing out. We'd love to help you."*

Of course, always sign off with your first name. Keep it personal.

After that, make sure you *keep in touch* with Tom, using automation or not. Don't forget about Tom, or he'll forget about you.

When you use my conversion process end to end with all the right digital assets in place, up to 70% of your PC's will turn into VIP's.

So what about the other 30%?

Well, not everyone will be the right fit for you. Not everyone will be ready to buy and so on. But it's critically important to keep in touch with them all. Make sure they're on your database and that you continue to serve them up value, and continue to deepen their advocacy for your brand.

The "done for you" way to conversion.

I use the value approach in everything I do at *The Strategic Bookkeeper, so* I'm not afraid to toot my own horn and tell you what you get when you join my program. In fact, it would be remiss of me not to tell you, because you could end up doing a whole lot of work you don't need to do. And that might risk wasting your time and delaying your success.

So, to serve you best I'm going to tell you as often as I can what's done for you in the program – and anything else I think is pertinent to your journey.

If you're thinking about joining my program, it's important for you to know that the assets required for the conversion process have already been created for you, and you can start using them immediately. This includes Ignition software templates, a pricing calculator, your guarantee, brochures, website pages, scripts, videos and more.

So let's move on to *Succession*, which will be a lot of fun!

Chapter 6. The Joy of Succession.

Up until now we've concentrated on the process of creating your brand and the assets that support it, followed by ways to find clients (or to help them find you), and bring them on board.

Now we get to the bedrock of the methodology – the succession techniques that will help you lock in clients for the long term. By taking them on a journey from core products to "Succession Products".

Applied correctly, succession can help future-proof your business from the threats of automation and cheap overseas labour, which is taking up more and more of the "traditional bookkeeping", or straight bookkeeping market.

Why future-proof?

Kodak was founded in the late 1880s, became a giant in the photography industry in the 1970s and filed for bankruptcy in 2012. For almost a hundred years, Kodak owned film and photo space.

However, in the late 1980's analogue started its decline and digital started its incline which of course, continued. Despite the fact that it had been an Eastman Kodak engineer who'd built the first ever digital camera in 1975, Kodak refused to adapt (aka: future proof) believing that it wasn't necessary. In 1991 they finally released a digital camera, but it was too late & they filed for bankruptcy in 2012.

Don't be like Kodak.

The key to your future is in succession.

Succession is the way to live your dream on your terms – a goal that is a lot harder to reach doing just straight, traditional bookkeeping than it is doing strategic bookkeeping with succession services.

The truth is that what we can reasonably charge for straight bookkeeping is, on its own, not a sustainable way to build a thriving practice. It's a "job" at best. The bottom line is, when you include succession product lines, you'll run a healthier, more profitable practice. And you'll delight your clients more.

You can and should charge more for succession products than straight bookkeeping.

Bookkeeping is a bit of a grudge purchase – a cost that most clients don't understand is really an investment. But, like marketing, Strategic Bookkeeping is an investment, not a cost. Because it generates a return greater than the spend.

If your mind is somewhat blown right now, then good! Because I'm asking you to make a fundamental shift in your thinking. I'm asking you to consider charging a lot more for strategic services. Like, two and a half to ten times more. Say what?

Rinse and repeat time: let's make your current ceiling your new floor.

One thing to note and note well: I am not advocating for ripping clients off! I am advocating valuing yourself and avoiding your own Kodak moment.

The power of accountability.

I used to think that once a client turned their business around, they didn't need to meet with me monthly anymore. Oh, how wrong I was.

Now I know, and actually my clients continually tell me, that continuing to hold them accountable to their numbers and to the actions they need to take, is one of the most impactful parts of what we do.

When I started engaging my clients in my strategic succession services, they went from being "happy with our service" but still ultimately feeling like it was a grudge purchase, to saying things like this:

"I don't care about the fee, I can't do this without you."

"I once thought I couldn't afford a 'you', now I know I can't do without you."

"I have no idea how to quantify the value of this service – it is certainly far in excess of the fee! Working strategically makes me focus on the opportunities that have previously slipped past me. We get so busy with the day to day running and growth in a business that the obvious is often hidden. Time with Jeannie secured the respite that was needed to see a better way and the result has been huge gains in profitability over 100% in under three months. Ecstatic with the outcome."

Succession is about mindset.

If "straight bookkeeping" has been your comfort zone to date, then this is the part where I'm going to ask you to step out it. I've met a lot of bookkeepers who are reluctant to go beyond straight bookkeeping and begin to investigate the numbers with their clients.

If that's you, it's time to ask yourself why. Is there any real reason or is it "shame and vulnerability".

A lesson in psychology.

People rarely buy what they actually need. They buy what they want or what they believe they need – which is exactly what you have to be there to sell them. If you try to sell your VIP's what you *know* they need, rather than what they *believe* they need, you'll lose them.

In my experience most new clients require catch up and rectification work of some description, and once that's done, they require either an ongoing Bookkeeping Package or DIY Bookkeeping Package.

At this point, in our experience, you can, and you should give them a choice of three packages – one with "straight bookkeeping" and the other two including succession products – which is what this chapter is all about.

As you'll learn, succession products deliver much higher value to you and your clients.

A Ted Talk digression.

If you haven't already listened to the amazing Brené Brown's Ted Talks about shame and vulnerability, take a few minutes to do so now. Brené is a researcher, and she has found that embracing shame and vulnerability is a key to success.

Shame is the voice that says, "you're never good enough" and, if you dare to challenge it, that responds with, "who do you think you are?" Brené says that the antidote to shame is empathy – one of our five conversion qualities as noted above.

Vulnerability is about being physically and emotionally open to uncertainty and risk. What it is not, is weakness.

As bookkeepers (and this applies to accountants as well) we're not particularly comfortable with "not having all the answers," and it's in our nature to want to know what to expect – but when we understand where our shame and vulnerability around that discomfort comes from, we can overcome it. Please listen to Brené.

Let me tell you a secret.

Are you ready? Here it is: you have all the skills and aptitude to investigate the numbers. Because if I can do it, so can you. I'm not a rocket scientist – yes, I'm an intelligent human being, but no more or less than you.

I've been investigating the numbers since I was fresh out of my Certificate 4 in Bookkeeping, and I would go as far as to say that it might be easier than some of the "straight bookkeeping" work you do. How's that for a mindset shift!

And the great thing is, you'll learn more and more as you grow in this space – and I promise it will be fun and interesting.

A lesson from the Wizard of Oz.

In our industry, I've often felt a bit like the Dorothy in the Wizard of Oz – surrounded by bookkeepers with far more skills than confidence. Just like the lion already had courage, the scarecrow already had a brain, and the tin man already had a heart, you already have everything you need to succeed at succession.

Succession is also about questions.

When you're setting out to investigate your client's numbers, the real value you bring to the process is the questions you ask. Your client is the expert in their business – whether they're a plumber or digital marketing consultant or a retailer or whatever. It's not your job to be an expert in their field, it's your job to ask questions that shine a light on their numbers.

Sure, you might collaborate with your client on some answers, and you will definitely educate them plenty along the way. But what I'm about to show you is not about having all the answers - it's far more about asking questions. You'll see what I mean as we dive into some of my succession products.

Lead lines for Succession.

As we discussed in conversion, lead lines – or as I call them welcome lines – can be a powerful tool in turning a PC into a VIP. In succession, they're a tool to take the VIP on a journey from core products to succession products.

Use these primary lead lines in order to gain maximum succession success:

Diagnostics – the 15-minute Business Health Check.

The same quiz you use for prospects will usually suffice. Our "done for you" asset in this space has 17 questions that dive deep into how well your VIP's know and use their numbers. One of the great things about this welcome line is that it leads the participant into a kind of self-assessment space where they become aware of the problems and opportunities with just a little help from you. So they really feel as if they've started to accomplish something.

The objective is to provide them with a bit of general information about their score, and encourage them to book a complimentary consultation. That's where you'll review their results and give them personalised recommendations.

It's all about value.

The business health check is about seeking to understand your client's problems and their knowledge levels and being of service. Your services are the solution – and that's not a sales pitch, it's just a fact.

How it works.

The process is simple – text or call your client and ask them if you can have 15 minutes of their time on phone or zoom. Let them know that your aim is to learn more about their business so you can understand how to serve them best. They will be grateful for your interest and concern.

You conduct the health check itself as a dialogue, which will naturally lead to lots of "ah ha" moments for you both. As I said, our health check checklist has 17 questions, so be sure you have the right questions handy.

As you go along, you might find yourself saying, "this is amazing, I'm learning so much about your business. What do you think?" At the end, ask them straight out how valuable they found the health check.

Then, say, "You know Tom, I'd really like to dive a little deeper to really help you kick some goals. Would you be interested in making some time for a complimentary Planning & Strategy Session?"

Tom might want to know what that's all about, so tell him "Well, it takes an hour or so. It follows a set agenda so that I can help you look at where you are now, where you want to be and how to get there." Then book him in.

Rinse and repeat time.

Whenever you make a meeting and you set a time limit, stick to it. Respect for your PC's or VIP's time is absolutely sacred. You've allocated 15 minutes for the business health check, so keep your promise. If you think you need to go over, seek permission or book another time to continue the conversation.

A diagnostics success story.

Not so long ago I did a "prosperity" health check with one of my long-standing VIP's. They've been with me for a few years, and it's been quite a journey. They've trusted me and bought into my whole kit and kaboodle (including our online courses and resources) which they tell me is an incredible tool kit.

Over the space of two years we'd helped them get clarity around their profit and cash to a point where we were all like, "ok, this is great, you've done it".

At that point I said, "ok, the profit and cash is there, now let's talk about prosperity. Which is about being time rich and around purpose and legacy."

I asked both participants to score their prosperity "now" and how it's changed from their "then". They both scored a 6 for their "now" and a 1 for their "then". Amazing.

This diagnosis did two amazing things. Firstly, it helped them see how far they'd come – progress! Secondly it helped us understand more about what we needed to work on next which was freeing up their time.

The tools and processes we used in that situation are exactly the same as those I provide for the members of my program, with all the checklists and other material ready to go - done-for-you. That's something to know if you're thinking about joining.

Annual Planning & Strategy Session

I offer all my clients one 90-minute Annual Planning & Strategy Session as a value add to their ongoing bookkeeping services, and I believe that it should conservatively cost around $1000 for my IP, acumen and time. Yes, I value the heck out of myself and this strategy session is incredibly high value.

It's a genuine offer, aimed at helping my clients step away from the busy work of "doing" and spend important time on planning, which we all know is a key driver to success. If you fail to plan, you plan to fail right?

During the session I focus on these things:

- What's happening for you right now (in business and in life)?
- Give it a score out of 10 – 1 being can't pay the bills, 10 being the sweet life.
- What's the main reason for your score?
- And how does that make you feel?
- Now, what does 10/10 look like?

- Where do you want to be in the future?
- When do you want to get there – is it a year from now? Two? Three? Five? Ten???
- During our Q&A, I help them create an action plan, which comes naturally with this form of enquiry
- What's your motivation to move the needle to get to your 10/10 life?
- Would you like me to show you how I could help you move from your X out of 10 to your 10/10?

Of course, they'll answer yes, so your response is to show them your menu. Talk naturally about how you can help them improve their score and what that could mean for their business.

On the off chance that they're not motivated to "move the needle", ask them why. What's the main reason for that? You might find it's fear or they feel alone and unsupported. When you seek to understand, the answers you find can surprise you.

More welcome lines.

My eBook, *The 7 deadly cashflow sins*, is not only a great lead line into succession products for clients, it's an excellent educational resource for you too. Just another one of the "done for you" assets we'll provide you if you join The Strategic Bookkeeper Transformation Program and become part of my tribe.

In addition, I created my "better in business" podcast as a lead line for all Strategic Bookkeepers who join my program. That was a big effort for just one practice, but when you consider its power for the whole tribe, it was worth it.

Along with our two main succession welcome lines, we have a package of very rounded out assets we give our members in our program. They're powerful in principle and effective in action, so we spend time working with you on education, implementation and support to ensure you get results.

Taking the next step – Succession Products.

The succession welcome lines are about educating the client as to what they really need and making them really want to take the next step into succession products.

Back in *A lesson in psychology*, I mentioned once a new client's catch up and rectification work is complete, you should give them a choice of three packages – one with "straight bookkeeping" and the other 2 including succession products.

I have two nice and easy succession products that you can offer your clients first up, and they are

- A workshop.
- A monthly or quarterly meeting.

The workshop.

This is a one-off workshop to get them started on the right foot – to make the monthly or quarterly meetings more effective and productive.

There are three parts to your "workshop product":

- Pre-work by you, in which you spend some time diving into the VIP's financials
- The meeting – where you spend about an hour workshopping the numbers with your client.
- Post-work – some time spent attending to the issues raised in the meeting and wrapping it all up.

The actual time it takes overall will vary client to client and we're not charging for time, we're charging for outcomes.

"A Strategic Bookkeeper prices outcomes and value, not time. She invests in and values herself, her skills, her IP, her experience"

Productise this service by giving it a name and a fixed price investment which I recommend is between $897 and $1997 for this initial workshop. At the time of writing this book we are charging $997.

And I'm willing to bet that for that investment – for a product that is very impressive in its scope and outcomes – is less than what your clients will find in ways to save or make money thanks to your input and help.

The bookkeepers bet.

A great way to develop your succession services and practice them is to make "The Bookkeepers Bet". Pick a client and ask them if you can make them a bet. Say, "I bet I can save or make you more than $1000 *in profit or cash* in the space of about an hour – and if you'll have this bet with me, I won't even charge you for it."

If you do make this bet and win, make sure you quantify the win and ask them if they'd like to keep optimising their profit and cash month on month. There should be absolutely no reason you can't sign them up to this same workshop (and charge for it). There's massive value in repeating the process and what you'll find is your focus will shift and they'll get massive value all over again. Alternatively, sign them up for monthly numbers mastery meetings.

If that all sounds a bit scary (because of your bookkeeper psychology) take some of the guesswork out by hand picking a client whose profit and loss makes the most sense to do this exercise with:

- A client who you know could put $1000 in the bank with smarter collections.
- A client who could quite obviously consolidate or cut costs.
- A client who could benefit from Q & A around revenue or cost of sales, to make or save money.

You have access to all their numbers – you're standing on a mountain of incredible information that most other business owners would give their right arm to access – use it to benefit your clients.

Monthly or quarterly meetings.

If you're already providing your clients with monthly reports, great. But in all my years as a Bookkeeper in Practice, I haven't seen one client disciplined enough to sit down every month and do the work required that will ultimately optimise their profit and cash.

Let's face it, most of them simply lack the know-how anyway.

And that's why they need you – to shine a light on their financials monthly, to hold them accountable to what's actually going on in their business, and what they need to do next.

The numbers tell the story – and you are the storyteller.

Adam, my local cafe owner, pulled $300k more profit out of his business by working his numbers. Prior to that he was stuck in the "busy work" of running the cafe – now he says, "it's all about the numbers".

The mechanics of these regular meetings.

The meeting/workshop process itself is fairly straightforward. You sit down with your client and review their financials – their:

- Profit and loss (tip: I recommend you look at their profit and loss using "total" rather than "year to date", and over a rolling 12-month period so you can see trends month to month – this is a great view).
- Aged payables and aged receivables.
- Balance sheet etc

And as with every meeting you have with any VIP, you ask questions. "Why are there 10 sales invoices overdue?" "Why did revenue spike so much last month" "Are these costs standard to your industry?". Seek to understand, seek to help, seek to give value.

Script it first.

If you start with a script or agenda, it will get easier and easier to get through them every time. Here's an approach we use with great success:

> "Before we get started, I'd like to explain the *what, why* and *how* of these meetings. We're going to be addressing a number of issues here, and I need your commitment to be accountable in this process. Because we know that successful business owners know their numbers. Here's what we'll examine in the session:
>
> - Review – together we're going to open your books and look at your numbers.
> - Questions – what we find in your books will lead to both you and I asking questions.
> - Answers – it's on both of us to answer honestly and as fully as we can. What we can't answer now we promise to answer later.
> - Targets – we'll look at what targets you need to set for sales, and gross and net profit.
> - Results – and we'll look at how your results stacked up against those targets.

- Action Plan – all of this will generate a need for actions, so we'll create an action plan that I need you to commit to.

And then, next month when we meet again, I'm going to ask you if you've taken the actions promised – there's that accountability once again. How does all that sound?"

The cost

I recommend you charge between $200 and $500 for a monthly meeting – or, if you're offering it quarterly, $300 to $500 per quarter, because it will take longer.

Why charge more for quarterly? Why not? Which leads me into a quick digression into Bookkeeper mindset and pricing...

Your pricing system, your strategy simply cannot be a simple math equation to calculate time for money. Nor can it be with solely the client in mind. Your pricing system must first serve to ensure the financial health of your practice.

As you'll one day learn, when I launch The Healthy Bookkeeper - putting yourself first is the only way you can serve anyone.

If you fail to create a financially healthy practice that can sustain paying staff, continual education for you and your team, product innovation, license, insurances etc then you won't be able to serve your clients nearly as well as they deserve.

Other succession services.

These are the simplest and easiest succession services to start with, but the sky's the limit. What else are you secretly skilled at? What else are you passionate about?

Go away and workshop the "one time" and "recurring" services that you could productise and solve problems with, to put into your succession suite of services.

The simplest example of a piece of IP that you could create and sell is a course. Build it once and there you have it – a high value piece of IP you can sell alone or bundle in with other services. Other examples include videos, books, systems, and guides.

My eBook The *7 deadly cashflow sins* is a perfect example of a piece of intellectual property that, yes, took me some time and effort to create, but now it's an asset that I can use forever. Not only that, used as a succession welcome line, it helps to future-proof my practice.

To say we've done a lot of work on succession products and strategies in The Strategic Bookkeeper Transformation Program is an understatement. If you're thinking about joining us, it's important to know that the assets, the systems, the support – everything you need to launch and follow through with succession products – is all done for you and ready to go.

Going next level – Selling your IP.

Before we finish with Succession, let's go back to where we started – the psychology of it and the mental barriers to success that I know you can overcome. Part of you is no doubt wondering, "Me, a bookkeeper, selling my IP?"

Think about unicorn companies like Google. What makes them successful?

They build an audience, and because they're selling ideas not just services, they have the potential to go global rather than remain local. That's what you're about to do too!

I get it, you're not going global with your bookkeeping services, although you could – I have a friend who operates in several countries. But if you're not already, you could easily be working with clients all over the country by the end of this lap of the sun.

The ideology shift.

I get it. To grasp IP as a high value product that you can sell your clients requires a paradigm shift – "a shift in your system of ideas, especially ones which form the basis of your economic theory".

Your current *bookkeeping economic theory* is time for money – even if you're value bundling, selling first line succession products or advisory services, they all require an input of time for the exchange of money.

IP as the basis of your economic theory is a whole new world – one where time for money is almost non-existent. Sure, there may be an investment of time at the beginning to create the IP, but that's it. Beyond that there's literally no cost of sales – no 'time for money' equation.

Bundling your IP.

As with all your succession products, bundling IP with other services gives you a competitive advantage because it increases the actual and perceived value of your services.

The rise of online courses.

I know that this section, on selling IP, will be the biggest mind-shift I'm asking you to make, but the good news is that you have time. Even though the rise of online courses since the pandemic is astronomical, it's still early days on this front in our industry.

Dipping your toe in this water now is adopting early, rather than adapting when it's too late and having your own personal Kodak moment – ouch.

Where do you start?

Like I said before, the sky's the limit. But for now, let's start at ground zero with some simple ideas that you can actually implement.

- *How to videos*: What could you do a short "how to" video about that would be useful to your clients?Here are three examples straight off the top of my head:
  - How to reserve money for your tax obligations.
  - How to read financial reports.
  - How to improve your cash flow
- *Short Courses* – could you create a short course for clients? *If you really want to learn something, teach it.* Even by reading this book you've learned so much – what do you know that you could teach in a short course?
- *Shared Google Drives, Documents & Sheets* - Forget email tennis, capture your IP and make it available to your clients in shared folders, sheets and documents. You'll be surprised at how quickly you can build a valuable library of your own intellectual property.

Yes, there is work involved in creating your own catalogue of IP. If you're thinking about joining The Strategic Bookkeeper Transformation Program, we'll provide you with IP to sell and bundle in with your services.

How I can help.

Now I want to tell you how I can help you. Because I know that developing and selling IP is a big shift, I want to give you a "done for you" option.

I'm all about the power of a tribe. Which is why I decided to develop a whole raft of IP that we could all sell. I thought "wait a minute, rather than all of us making this massive effort to understand what to create and then create it – which I've already done – I could simply offer all my stuff to bookkeepers all over the world so they can benefit and their clients can benefit too".

And actually, that's the approach that's at the heart of all my stuff – leverage. One for the benefit of many. I've developed an online academy that you'll have access to - you'll be able to sell stand-alone courses or bundle them in with your services. We even provide a world class marketing strategist to write your sales copy in order to enrol your clients.

On to success!

Succession is what will turn your bookkeeping practice into a growing strategic bookkeeping practice. It's the last major step in the progression that begins with brand, menu, attraction and conversion, and it highlights just how crucial it is that you get each of those steps right.

But there's still a couple of essential elements to your success, so let's move onto them now – Systems and Team.

Chapter 7. The Beauty of Systems.

The way I look at it, first and foremost, systems are what we use to ensure we keep our promises to our clients. I use “systems” and “standard operating procedures (SOP)” interchangeably here, so when you see “systems” think SOP.

One of the things we love about systems or standard operating procedures is that they have a narrow purpose. They’re rigid and predictable, and they help staff recreate standardised services, so they contribute to the quality of the services you deliver. Robust and well thought out systems also mitigate risk by:

- ✓ Reducing the potential for errors.
- ✓ Keeping costs low.
- ✓ Managing client expectations.
- ✓ Eliminating nasty surprises.

A little background.

When we win work, we make promises via our service level agreement. And if you can't keep your promises to your clients, your business will fall apart. Not delivering on your promises means you won't get referrals and you won't retain clients, and your reviews are not likely to be stellar.

So if you plan to grow or take on staff, you're going to need robust systems in place that ensure everything goes according to your principles when you're not there. Let me tell you my story, because it's a great example of the *why* of systems.

My background with systems.

I've been involved in building and maintaining standard operating procedures (aka systems) for decades, in several different industries. I have dazzled and delighted by creating systems impacting customer satisfaction, profit margins and cash flow. I'm also a certified trainer and assessor, which means I understand adult learning styles and the value of using assessments in systems.

And so, with a strong foundation in all of this, when I got my first staff member, I systemised.

Prior to bringing on my first staff member *I was the system* and so my BAM (bare ass minimum) systems consisted mainly of checklists for end of period to ensure I didn't miss anything.

I am a proud person when it comes to my work standards, and early on, when critiques were given, I listened (as feedback is my fuel) and then I improved my checklists and my systems overall.

You see I believe that the best time and place to systemise is "on the job" – which I'll elaborate on later.

I soon got busy enough to bring on my first staff member. I knew I needed more than checklists, so I went about the task of documenting everything end-to-end, starting with the critical client workflows.

Once I had those all nutted out, I put together the requisite HR information, and then I wrapped it all up with an induction – including assessments. I didn't document sales, marketing, finance or administration processes until some years later.

This early investment in my business is key part of how I scaled – how I went beyond my f*ck up years and reached a point where I could choose my own adventure and live my dream on my terms. In retrospect, I had to endure those "f*ck up years", because there was still so much more to learn and perfect and implement.

As a Bookkeeper in Practice it's natural for you to think that systems are the be all and end all, because it's part of your profile. You naturally bias that way. But what you need, to build a thriving practice with delighted clients in order to be able to live your dream on your terms, is much more than systems.

You need to nail Brand, Menu, Attraction, Conversion, Succession, Systems and Team.

And none of that is static. Which is another reason I'm so passionate about The Strategic Bookkeeper Transformation program – because it's not static. It's not a set of manuals or a course on its own. It's a program, it's a tribe, and it's assets, and importantly it keeps moving and changing and growing with you and with our industry.

My competitors who sell franchise and license systems often focus more on *systems around quality and team* than they do on the end-to-end detail that I've gone into with my 7 key principles. What they offer around sales and marketing is often more general than specific with little to no focus on the powerful assets required. This often leads to lacklustre results and leads many bookkeepers to question what they're doing wrong or worse... their worth.

Systems and Team in The Strategic Bookkeeper Transformation program.

In the early days of developing my secret sauce I didn't think too much about systems and team. Not because they're not important, but because in all honesty, they're easier to nut out and nail. I knew that the first 5 principles in my method were much more difficult for bookkeepers to understand and master. I knew that bookkeepers needed more detail, more specifics around sales and marketing.

Sweat the small stuff.

If I could give you one piece of advice around systems, it's to "sweat the small stuff."

I'm an easy-going kind of person, and it's not in my nature to sweat the small stuff. But when it comes to your Standard Operating Procedures you really have no choice.

Because your processes are like soufflé recipes – they need to be followed carefully, precisely to get the desired results. If you miss any ingredient or step, or if you mess with a soufflé recipe, you simply turn out "fallen" soufflés. And nobody wants that.

A couple of valuable resources.

Systems are systems. To be honest, in all my years building and maintaining SOP's, not much has changed except the tech. The rules of the game remain the same. So rather than reinvent the wheel on systems, I'm going to point you to a really great "how to guide" which I recommend you read.

The Business Playbook by Chris Ronzio which you can find here: https://www.thebusinessplaybook.com/[7], is from the mind of the creator of "Trainual", our preferred SOP software. We love his work and recommend Chris.

If you want more:

- *The E-Myth* by Michael E Gerber
- *Systemology* by David Jenyns – click https://www.systemology.com/book/[8] for a link.

are both great books on systems.

[7]URL: www.thebusinessplaybook.com/
[8]URL: www.systemology.com/book/

Critical drivers for sales and marketing.

I've given you sales and marketing systems in this book, and I continue to explore these with you in my podcast, on my social media and more. Plus of course, in my program if you join my tribe.

What really makes these systems work is critical drivers – which we first talked about in the Keep in Touch marketing (KIT) section in *Chapter 4 – the Power of Attraction.* To rinse and repeat, these are the actions you do every day in a methodical way, to drive the results you want.

Let's say your target is two new and two upgraded clients per month. It seems quite a modest target, but two new and two upgraded clients per month would translate into over $250k of revenue and more than $150k in profit. Critical drivers are how you get there. And let me tell you right now, this is all highly achievable – I once set a target to generate one new enquiry per day and I did it.

To rinse and repeat again, let's make your current ceiling your new floor.

The system doesn't work – you work the system.

The way you work my sales and marketing systems, is by creating and relentlessly implementing and executing your critical drivers – the activities that will drive sales of your core and succession products.

I recommend you create a document or sheet, put it up on your wall and commit to doing your critical drivers daily.

- Use your succession lead lines.
  - Can you call/text one client per day to ask them for 15 minutes of their time to find out more about their business so you can serve them better?
  - Or maybe book that planning and strategy session with a client who's already done their health check?
- Follow up.
  - Make sure you're following up on proposals sent, but not accepted yet.
- EAP activities.
  - Could you reach out to a new potential partner?
  - Get in touch with an existing EAP to farm the relationship?

- Database and KIT activities.
    - Who could you quickly and easily keep in touch with?
    - For example, let's say you served a client on a catch up, but for whatever reason, you didn't migrate them to "ongoing". You could message them... "Hi Lisa, you just popped into my mind and I thought, I wonder if Lisa is keeping up to date – how's it all going?"

All of these activities are actually good manners – which is why I refer to some advocacy marketing activities "manners marketing". As my father always said, "never forget your customers and they'll never forget you."

He also said "Jeannie, everyone is a potential customer, so treat everyone as if they are a customer." It's great advice, because it reminds you to always have your manners on.

Don't limit yourself to these critical drivers, brainstorm your own – if not enough customers is your problem and you have the time, the more daily critical driver activities you do, the greater your results will be. I know this to be 100% true because I've tried and tested it all myself.

Capacity and waitlists.

Your system has a capacity, beyond which it will start to fail. If you don't have capacity and you say yes to doing the job, you might be making promises you can't keep. That's why you need to check your capacity to do the work when you do your needs analysis.

Of course, reaching capacity can be a good thing as long as you manage it properly. When we hit capacity, we instigate the use of a waitlist, which actually creates more demand. Because that's how scarcity works in business.

We try and keep waitlists to a month – a bookkeeper's cycle, so to speak, and we've never lost a client due to putting them on the waitlist. This system has worked incredibly well for me for over 10 years.

We use Google Calendar to check and manage capacity and schedule jobs – we also schedule all our jobs in *Xero Practice Manager.*

Time, tasks and deadlines.

Time management is one of your most critical systems, and in this regard technology is your friend.

We use *Xero Practice Manager* and *Precision by DEXT* to manage all our jobs, clocking time and tasks and managing deadlines across jobs in XPM, and lodging all tax compliance through *Xero Tax,* which is attached to it.

We implemented *Precision by DEXT* a few years ago, which was a big leap forward in terms of task management. Prior to that, we used *Xero Practice Manager* exclusively to manage tasks, backed up by manual checklists. That was a reasonable solution, but *Precision* offered us so much more – including the opportunity for massive efficiency gains.

We've been able to reduce our team (by natural attrition) while taking on more work, and we've reduced the number of keystrokes we make. Every tap on a keyboard costs you money, so every tap saved saves you money.

Efficiency gains.

I do feel the need to elaborate a bit here, because efficiency gains are something I learned the value of the hard way through years in practice.

Depending on where you are in your bookkeeping practice journey, "efficiency gains" might not mean much to you. So if this is your first lap around the sun on the subject, then listen up now. Let it marinate and observe it all in the real world so that it makes more sense over time.

Efficiency gains is simply about becoming more efficient in every area of your business over time. Efficiency gains lead to time and money saved – which leads to increased gross and net profit.

You should aim to gain efficiency in every department in your business – marketing, sales, client work, operations, administration, finance and HR.

Trust me now and believe me later, a more efficient you is a win for your clients too.

Streamlining workflows.

A few years ago, we adopted *Ignition* software (formerly known as *Practice Ignition*) which has led to efficiency gains as well. Like *Precision*, *Ignition* has transformed tasks into workflows, which is game changing, because everything just gets easier, more streamlined and efficient.

It automates a huge range of processes like payments and billing, proposals and engagement letters, and a whole heap of different tasks.

Using *Ignition,* we've been able to streamline the conversion process, improved conversion rates, improved uptake of succession services, and made authorities and terms and conditions a breeze.

Administration & Finance.

Ignition manages all of our client payments and integrates with *Xero*, reducing double handling while allowing customised billing for all of our VIP's.

We also use *Google Workspace (the GSuite)* extensively, including to collaborate on sheets and documents. We use *Gmail* for email, and their chat app features to turbo charge our internal communication and manage tasks that don't fit into *XPM* or *Precision*.

All this tech sounds daunting, but we'll teach you everything you need to know in The Strategic Bookkeeper Transformation program if you join the tribe. We go through all the detail and support you to integrate it so it makes running your practice easy.

My top tips for creating your Standard Operating Procedures.

It's a tech-oriented world these days, and we're lucky to live in a time when there are so many great apps and software platforms that can help you maximise efficiency and minimise waste. The software platform made for systems we use is *Trainual*, and I can highly recommend it. If you join my program, we provide you with done-for-you SOP's in Trainual and teach you how to use them.

My top tips - which Trainual is built to help you do

- Start systemising before you get your first staff member:
  - Start with the critical client workflow.
  - Document what you're doing while you're doing it.
  - Use videos – when I surveyed my team 50% of us preferred video instructions and the other half preferred written instructions – so do both!
  - Make sure to use checklists wherever appropriate – many of which are integrated into the tech these days.

- Create an Induction
  - Share the big picture: tell your team about yourself and your brand. This will make a huge difference to how your team delivers on the promises you make and how they perform overall.
  - *The Business Playbook* by Chris Ronzio that I've recommended you read dives into this in depth.
  - Include assessments – they turn information into training and are the 20% that makes 80% of the difference. *Trainual* know this, which is why they've built assessment into their software.
  - Assessments should be "open book" – the trainee is prompted to answer questions by referring back to the system – the action of typing the answer out while re-absorbing the material actually creates the learning. That's the Training and Assessment method.
  - I've tested inducting and training staff with and without assessments, and there's no comparison – assessments turbo charge their learning.
- A few tips and hints:
  - Only document what you're doing, not what you're *not* doing. Create a wish

list if you like, but *do not* put it in your process if you're not doing it right now.

- Don't teach – your system is not the place to teach someone how to be a bookkeeper, it's the place to teach a bookkeeper how to do things your way.
- Don't overcomplicate your systems – don't get bogged down in tech or process maps and flowcharts. I've been there, I've tried all the tech, I've tried process maps and flow charts and been down the over-complicating rabbit hole – benefit from my experience
- If you intend to remain a solo operator, using documents for SOP's is fine, but you'll still need tech for operations (like time, tasks, deadlines, and QA).
- If you're going to hire team, start as you mean to go on – invest in *Trainual* and explore the other tech tools I've recommended.

Technology as a succession product.

A dual benefit of *Trainual* is that they also have a Certified Consultant Program, which we jumped at because we recognised that we could productise services around systems for our clients.

And that's important because while we recognise that our clients all need systems, unlike us, they're not built to understand how to put them all together. We seized the opportunity to make *Trainual* consulting services a part of our succession suite – and you can do that too. But *Trainual* isn't the only provider whose systems can be adapted as succession products – *Dext* does it too.

Systems for Clients.

Part of our Strategic Foundation is that we want to work with clients who follow the systems we give them – and that's non-negotiable.

One of these systems is *Prepare by DEXT* – formerly known as receipt-bank. It's an automation and AI app that does the grunt work around keying bills (it does a lot more, but that's primarily what we use it for). As with most tech, we've tried alternatives and found *Prepare* to be the Rolls Royce.

We aim for 80% "hands free" coding – that's right, the tech is so accurate and efficient it does 80% of the data entry for us. It requires a little work up front, but then we reap the rewards in efficiency gains forever.

If you're thinking about cash-coding bills and expenses, don't (with the exception of catch-up work, then do!). A Strategic Bookkeeper's best practice is to capture bills in their entirety for the most informative accrual data outputs – which you'll need when you investigate the numbers. And *Prepare* does all that with automation and AI – beautifully.

Becoming a Strategic Bookkeeper is about meaningful data – not just accurate data –which is a big part of numbers strategy. In that realm, cash coding to manage progress bookkeeping is garbage – and we all know the old saying, "garbage in, garbage out."

Other systems our clients use.

Our clients interact with *Ignition* and *Xero Practice Manager*, and they collaborate with us in *Google sheets and documents*. When they follow the systems we give them, VIP's find that everything just gets easier and more efficient – so they save time and money. And let me tell you this - no one ever gets sick of saving time or money.

Making it all work – Quality Assurance (QA).

At the beginning of this chapter, I spoke about your team needing to follow your systems as closely as you would follow a soufflé recipe. You need a way to ensure that's happening because – (to continue with the metaphor I used earlier) – unfortunately you can't just take their word for it until it turns out that their soufflé is floppy or burnt.

When you have a team of one or more, QA checking is a necessary evil, and this is where tech like *Precision by Dext come into their own.*

Before introducing *Precision*, QA used to be time consuming, and frankly a cost I'd rather not be incurring. *Precision* changed all that for us by giving us optics around QA as well as amazing efficiency gains. Honestly, thanks to *Precision*, I sleep better.

I'm more confident about our QA than ever before, because *Precision* allows us to see visually the health of every file, and track exactly where our team is up to in their monthly workflow (tasks).

Precision has allowed us to detect issues in team performance sooner rather than later, so we can implement performance management measures faster and more efficiently.

I'd recommend *Precision by Dext* to every bookkeeper, because it's such a massive time saver and such a great way to measure your QA. Even if you're flying solo, the diagnostics around file health are just dreamy.

Practicing what you preach.

It's not enough for us to insist that our VIP's play by our rules – we apply the same logic to our internal systems. We investigate our own numbers, we have financial targets, and we track team productivity carefully to maintain a robust, viable practice.

My right hand is my numbers coach, and she meets monthly with our whole team and conducts the very same "service" we provide our clients – we assess how our policies to drive productivity are going, we review our results, and we decide on an action plan.

We acknowledge our accomplishments, and we find ways to overcome our issues, and everyone feels valued and involved.

It's essential that every bookkeeper in practice does this, because profit and cash is like oxygen for a business – prioritise it above all else because if your business suffocates, you can't serve or help anyone. Not your clients, not your family and not yourself.

Involve your VIP's.

We also welcome the input of our clients. They know that we're always available for feedback and constructive criticism on how we operate.

We send them a survey as part of a regular process we call *better every month*, asking them how satisfied they are on a scale of 1-10 – 1 being abysmal and 10 being remarkable – and how likely they are to recommend us to others.

Asking that question is known as finding out your net promoter score, and it's one of the most important measures of a business's health and viability. Google "net promoter score" and find out ways you can ascertain and monitor yours.

I can't emphasise enough how important it is to a have a rhythm around activities like this. When it's an established part of the routine and everyone really contributes to it, it can be a powerful motivator for positive change. But it also breeds loyalty, productivity and pride.

It's a lot, I know.

Systems have become so much more tech-dependent in recent times, it's hard to keep up. And things change all the time. If you're thinking of joining The Strategic Bookkeeper Transformation program, we will give you done-for-you SOP's and help you with all the tech.

We treat systems and teams separately to the rest of our program and so you'll find a dedicated person on this, to work with you.

We will also be offering systems to buy stand-alone as we recognise that some bookkeepers actually want to start there.

Now, we're almost there but we have one more vital aspect of your business to discuss – your team.

Chapter 8. The Strength of Teams.

Now let's dive into the dynamics of your team. Even the smartest system in the world won't work well unless you have the right people in the right jobs and the right leadership for those people.

In other words, all your work in creating a brand and menu, and all your efforts in attraction, conversion and succession – everything relies on your team. At the end of the day, what really counts is the 5% activities that make all the difference.

It's all about leadership.

The first lesson is that you need to learn how to step up as a leader. Successful strategic bookkeepers educate themselves, and leadership is a skill you need to keep developing and polishing.

There's not much I would have done differently in my long journey to here, because in the end all those experiences – the good, the bad and the ugly – made me the accomplished bookkeeper in practice I am today. But if I had my time over, I would invest more in leadership education and strategies.

I would've continued to hire slow, but I would've fired a little faster. I would've tamed my people-pleasing monster. And I would go in understanding the difference between a leader and a manager, and when to be both.

Manager or Leader? Or both?

Leaders create the vision, communicate that to the tribe, and provide strategic direction around achieving the goals the vision creates.

Managers plan, staff, organise, direct and control.

And until you hire a manager you'll need to be both.

That's a big deal. Because as leader you need to share your vision with your manager and her team so they understand it, buy into it, and make it come to life. That means getting everyone on the same page and working with a singular purpose to build and promote your brand, your value proposition, strategic foundation and so on – for the benefit of your VIP's.

And as a manager you need to be a superstar – a self-starting critical thinker who makes no excuses and keeps the juggernaut rolling.

Invest in your skills.

Being successful as a leader and manager is a big key to building a thriving practice as a strategic bookkeeper. So it pays to invest in learning and refining your skills in both. Tune into podcasts, read books. Don't believe for one second that this stuff is easy because it's not. Many bookkeepers think of the "technical work" as the hard stuff, but when you have a team, your leadership and management can easily make or break your business.

My thoughts on leadership.

Once upon a time I read a book called *The One Thing* by Gary Keller and Jay Papasan, where they explore the idea that there's always one thing that if focused upon and got right, would make everything else easier.

And when it comes to team, that thing is trust.

That boils down to the difficult question you ask each and every team member – *can I trust you?* Now, I know that might seem offensive to ask and so, you don't need to actually ask them – you can simply ask yourself, here's how.

Trust at work is about punctuality and reliability – *"doing what you said you'd do in the timeframe you said you'd do it"*. For example...

- Completing tasks
- Meeting deadlines

Put another way, trust is about *"promises kept"*.

Fact: Organisations that have tracked and monitored "promises kept" have been able to increase their profits by up to 100%.

Of course, to earn your team's trust you need to lead by example and keep your promises too.

Share the big picture.

Your big picture is *why you exist*. Great organisations share their big picture with their team so they are:

- all on the same page
- working towards the same vision for their clients
- living their mission to achieve that vision
- ensuring the "detail" make sense

Of course, you'll first need to get clear on your big picture yourself so you can share it in an encouraging and empowering way – which is why this book has taken you through the steps you'll need to gain a powerful, innate understanding of your own motivations and reasons. Your brand, your strategic foundation, vision, mission and menu are all the things that make up your big picture, so by the time you get through your second reading of this book (in just a few pages now), you'll be ready to inspire and enrol others in your big picture.

How to be a good manager.

As a manager there are 5 key areas you'll need to focus on:

1. Plan.
2. Staff.
3. Organise.
4. Direct.
5. Control.

It's up to you to develop what they mean to you, and the trick is to learn and never stop learning.

Be practical.

You need to be totally up front about your expectations and obligations. Spell out your requirements in terms of KPIs, critical drivers and productivity levels, and be just as honest about what you offer in return. Do you allow flexibility in hours, bonuses, profit sharing or other incentives? Let your team know because such benefits are great for building loyalty and efficiency.

Superstars, workhorses, yo-yo's and time wasters.

As a leader and manager, you'll likely encounter four distinct types of team members – superstars, workhorses, yo-yo's and time wasters. Your practice will only live its full potential with superstars and workhorses on the team.

Workhorses are diligent hard workers who consistently complete their tasks and meet their deadlines. They respond well to leadership and work well with their manager.

Superstars can do all that, but they're also self-starting critical thinkers. In some ways, they're better than you are! And you love that about them. It should actually be your goal to recruit team members superior to yourself, because when you do that, your business will soar and you'll be freed up to lead rather than get bogged down in managing.

Yo-yo's are, as their name suggests, up and down. They might perform one day and be a nightmare the next. Consistency is what you're after, not peaks and troughs.

Time wasters are a drag on your practice. They waste their own time and the time of those around them, so they're actually toxic to your business.

Your people pleasing monster will want to give yo-yo's and time wasters another chance. Maybe you tell yourself that you can see their potential. But the solution here is, to rinse and repeat, hire slow and fire fast. Or bear the consequences of the damage they will do.

Zero Tolerance.

So, a new team member has been inducted and trained, and assessed as competent in your standard operating procedures. So the expectation is that they'll follow your systems to the letter, right?

But what if they don't?

Well first, there's no excuse. The only possible reason is that they simply decided not to make it a priority. In our SOP's we're crystal clear that if you get too busy you should sing out and management will reduce your workload. So busy isn't an excuse.

And when a team member doesn't deliver on a promise – which is what agreeing to abide by your SOP's is – then you can't deliver on your promises.

We guarantee our service level agreement or it's free, so our team must complete every task and meet all deadlines. It's non-negotiable.

Don't get brought undone by your people pleasing monster.

It's fine to develop friendships with your colleagues, but you need to be the boss first and a friend second. You need to be able to take the friend hat off swiftly and put the boss hat on. That's not easy, but at times it's necessary. If required, name it to tame it – say "to have this conversation I'm going to take my friend hat off and put my boss hat on, okay?"

Be tough – really tough if you have to – but fair. Hire slowly and methodically but don't be afraid to fire fast and fairly. And remember, tough but fair bosses who have great systems have very low staff turnover.

The "emotional bank account".

Imagine that each of your team members – including you – has an emotional bank account. To get the most out of your team, observe one simple rule: make three deposits into any individual's emotional bank account before making one withdrawal.

What that means is that you need to comment on what they're doing well three times or more before telling them what they need to improve. I've seen this work and I can tell you, developing this skill will help you get more out of your team

The "feedback sandwich".

Kind of similar to the emotional bank account, but for use in situations where negative feedback is necessary. Start with a positive, sandwich the negative, and end with a positive. "I like the way you did X, I think the way you do Y could be improved, and I love the way you do Z."

Performance Management

If a team member is not performing, you need to performance manage them. It might not feel nice, but you do have to do it. This is a time when you simply need to put the boss hat on, and be clear, be direct. Using your *feedback sandwich,* tell them what procedures and policies they aren't adhering to or administering well, and ask them to go back and retrain in them. Crucially, have them agree to comply.

Team Culture.

I believe the technique of developing a winning culture is quite misunderstood. In my experience, team culture is developed through strong, clear leadership, exceptional systems and good, strong management. I've seen it firsthand, and it works for me – but not just for me. One of my mentors is a 7-figure entrepreneur with little to no staff turnover in 18 years, and he has used this simple but effective formula to build his incredible team culture. So I know you can too.

The value of psychometric testing.

Psychometric testing is a powerful tool you should use as both a leader and a manager.

As a leader, it's about understanding your zone of genius and how you interact and communicate with others. It's about how to surround yourself with the right team.

As a manager, it's about understanding yourself and those you manage. This kind of knowledge is power, because you'll be able to use what you learn to support your team to win the game.

Tests you can try.

I recommend that you do the *Wealth Dynamics test* created by Roger Hamilton (wealthdynamics.com), and maybe the *DISC Profile* test (discprofile.com). Everyone on my team does and shares their *Wealth Dynamics* results, which is fun and rewarding for us all. Doing the test will help you understand what sort of work you need to do to develop your team and your own leadership skills.

Whether you're a Lord, a Deal Maker, a Creator, or a Star will affect how you choose, manage and deal with your team, so it's handy to know your *WD* profile. My right hand is a "mechanic" built for taking things apart and putting them back together better and stronger than before – which is why she heads up systems.

I don't decide on whether to hire someone until I have their *Wealth Dynamics,* and *DISC Profile* results, and I know whether they're a starter, maintainer or finisher.

Recruitment.

What are your recruitment processes like?

I have a long history in recruiting and training team across several industries, with decades of learning and experience behind me. And the biggest blunders I see in terms of recruiting the wrong people happen because of lack of process. Often because the business owner uses a "casual" approach. There can be nothing casual about how you recruit team!

You can find potential candidates anywhere, but when you do they must be put through your "recruitment process", and it must be systematic and rigorous. That's the key.

So what's the process?

Let's rinse and repeat with Abraham Lincoln – give me 6 hours to chop down a tree, and I'll spend the first 4 sharpening the axe. Or in this case, I spend considerable time creating a thorough Job Advertisement, which is really more like a position description. Because I'll the use it as the basis of the questionnaire I ask all candidates to complete.

We use *Google Forms* for our recruitment questionnaires. Candidates are instructed to use the form to answer a range of questions and upload their resume and other certificates. It's also the gateway platform we use to get them to do a *DISC Profile* test, and any other testing we deem necessary.

A great thing about giving candidates an instruction like this is assessing whether they follow it. If a candidate can't follow this simple instruction, will they really cut the mustard as a bookkeeper? I don't think so.

I do know that when we approach recruitment in this way we're able to find our top three candidates with ease.

The interview.

My favourite interview question is "Tell me about yourself".

Even though you've gathered a ton of information about the candidate already, ask this question. It's broad, it allows your candidate to share information about herself freely, and you'll get insights in her answers that won't come from more formal questions.

My next favourite question is "What questions do you have for me?" This is where we find out whether the candidate has done her homework on me and my practice, and gives an idea of her experience and aptitude for the job.

From there on in, your Job Ad and questionnaire results should form the basis for all other questions and conversations.

The final decision

Here's where things can get a little emotional – where our big-boss hat can start to slip off and our friend hat slip on.

You've had a great chat and discovered that you have things in common. Your people pleasing monster takes hold, and you're at risk of making an emotional rather than a rational decision. It's easy to do – I know because I've done it.

If that's you, don't be afraid to seek help or even delegate the final interview and selection stages. These days, 100%, I'm hands off on recruitment – I let my amazing process and people take care of this for me, and it works brilliantly.

At the time of writing this there's a massive skills shortage in Australia, so we recruit nationally rather than locally. Hot tip: if you advertise on *Seek*, add "work from home" in your job add title and it will appear nationally, even though you must choose a local location.

Should I outsource?

Has there ever been a hotter debate in our industry? As a bookkeeper, I feel like this subject is right up there with Politics and Religion. But here goes.

First off, you do not have to outsource to be a Strategic Bookkeeper – the choice is personal and entirely yours. But I will share my story, hoping it will help you as you create your own story.

I'm a future focussed person, and I find the changing economic and technology landscape fascinating. I believe the principle of "adapt or die" is almost a law in business and nature, and I don't fight it. I try and understand the changes coming, and find ways to adapt without compromising my values and beliefs. I should also remind you that money will never be my first priority. *"Money is the bi-product of doing something well and the positive impacts".*

I identified outsourcing early and so, given the above, I dabbled – but I did it "Jeannie style".

In about 2013 I hired a helper – a bookkeeper in the Philippines, who I sourced on *Upwork*. I didn't put her on client files, I actually used her as more of a VA to get a feel for how she did on our internal bookkeeping. I learned what did and didn't work, about the Philippines culture, and about using a *BPO (Business Process Outsourcing)* versus recruiting on *Upwork*. I decided that at some point, outsourcing was something I'd have to get more serious about. I would have to adapt or die.

Fast forward to 2017, when I implemented outsourcing as part of our overall team strategy. I was done with the testing – it was time to roll my sleeves up and future proof so I wouldn't have my own Kodak moment.

I know that some of you may be concerned about outsourcing taking local jobs, but to be honest I haven't seen evidence of that in our industry.

These days we live in a global economy with a global workforce, and I don't believe that's going to regress, I believe it's going to progress. Again, it's up to you, but through outsourcing we've been able to offer clients a greater level of service and at the same time have a greater impact on local and global communities.

Let's talk about productivity.

Productivity is something that you need to be mindful of at all times in your practice.

"Profit bleeds" mean you're losing money – and probably the biggest drain of all is being billed for non-billable hours by your bookkeeping team.

In my practice, any non-billable time, like when we have our weekly meetings, must be approved and is tracked.

Time tracking.

Although we charge a fixed price for most of what we do, we track the time clocked on jobs in order to compare it with budgets and determine job profitability. We aim for 66% or higher job profitability, and we use a traffic light system to visually represent this – green for 66% and above, orange below that, red below 50%.

As a system it's incredibly robust, and it keeps our team honest as well. It's transparent, and effective. As I've said before, we've come a long way to the point where we have turnkey systems. And you can access them as a member of our The Strategic Bookkeeper Transformation program.

Meet often, meet well.

Once you bring on a team, you increase the need for management – which takes time and in turn costs money. If your team has a forum to raise and discuss issues, suggest fixes and talk openly about problems, communication tends to flow well.

By implementing our *better every week* system to review your week in the rear-view and look out the windscreen at the week ahead, you'll get rid of unscheduled interruptions that can be a productivity killer. Another game changing system we developed along the way was to implement a meeting rhythm whereby "team reports to team". This allows you to step away and let your team monitor each other and themselves.

Meetings like this encourage your team to be accountable to and support one another, and the result is that overall, you'll minimise the "management" required.

Okay we're done.

I could go on about teams forever. But as I'm sure you've noticed, I could go on about every aspect of this crazy, beautiful, rewarding business of *being a strategic bookkeeper* forever and ever.

I'm sure that by now you've also noticed how deeply every aspect of our practice is connected with every other. Your strategic foundation feeds into your brand and your menu, which work together to create your attraction, conversion and succession strategies, and they all influence the way you create your systems and build your team.

It's a big, organic machine masterminded by you with a little help from me. It can and will be a rollercoaster at times, it's sure to excite you one day and scare you a little the next, but, by becoming a strategic bookkeeper, I think you'll love every minute of it. I know I have.

It's up to you now.

What if everything you ever wanted was just one decision away?

Becoming a Strategic Bookkeeper is the decision that can and will change your life – if you make it.

Use this book. Listen to the podcast. Enjoy the journey.

And I would love nothing more than for you to become a Strategic Bookkeeper by joining my program, so please feel free to express your interest here: https://www.thestrategicbookkeeper.global/wa itlist[1].

I am sure that working together we can help you live your dream on your terms, and give you the time and the financial success to chase your own adventures. I've proven it time and time again, and I'd love to show you how it will work for you.

Let's go!

Jeannie

1. https://www.thestrategicbookkeeper.global/wa itlist

Milton Keynes UK
Ingram Content Group UK Ltd.
UKHW020345280524
443152UK00008B/41